To Marjory

from

Robert Tims

19 April 1993.

MALVERN COLLEGE

Aerofilms and Aero-Pictorial Ltd

A HISTORY OF
MALVERN COLLEGE
1865 TO 1965

BY

RALPH BLUMENAU

M.A., B.Litt. (Oxon.)
Senior History Master
of Malvern College

★

WITH A FOREWORD BY
SIR JOHN WHEELER-BENNETT
K.C.V.O., C.M.G., O.B.E., Hon. D.C.L. (Oxon.), F.R.S.L.

LONDON
MACMILLAN & CO LTD
NEW YORK · ST MARTIN'S PRESS
1965

MACMILLAN AND COMPANY LIMITED
St Martin's Street London WC 2
also Bombay Calcutta Madras Melbourne

THE MACMILLAN COMPANY OF CANADA LIMITED
70 Bond Street Toronto 2

ST MARTIN'S PRESS INC
175 Fifth Avenue New York 10 NY

PRINTED IN GREAT BRITAIN

TO THE MEMORY
OF
'JUDY' PORCH

FOREWORD

SIR JOHN WHEELER-BENNETT,
K.C.V.O., C.M.G., O.B.E., Hon. D.C.L. (Oxon.), F.R.S.L.

THE future of the Public Schools lies upon the lap of the Gods, and it would be a bold man who at this juncture would essay a prophecy as to what that future may be. I have not that courage. But the past and the present of this system, which stands among the greatest of our national institutions, we may examine with comparative safety — at any rate from the historical point of view.

The system received its official parliamentary recognition by the Public Schools Act of 1868, but its origins lie much further back in the charitable concepts of such pious founders as William of Wykeham and King Henry VI. For centuries the seven great boarding-schools — Eton, Winchester, Charterhouse, Harrow, Rugby, Shrewsbury and Merchant Taylors', with the day-schools of Westminster and St. Paul's — were accepted without question as being as much an integral part of our national life as the Universities. For the last hundred years or more, however, the Public School system has become the subject of increasing criticism and controversy. By its supporters it is defended as a means whereby the best quality of academic education can be combined with an opportunity of developing character, earning self-reliance and encouraging loyalty and service to the community at the expense of self-interest. The critics attack the Public Schools as hotbeds of snobbery and prejudice, forcing grounds of class consciousness, where brains are subordinated to brawn ; a sort of Procrustean bed which all are made to fit by the simple process of lopping and stretching, with the consequent destruction of original thought and development. There were even those who shared the view of Oscar Wilde's 'Lady Bracknell' : 'Fortunately in England, at any rate, education produces no effect whatsoever. If it did, it would prove a serious danger to the upper classes.'

Not the least fascinating aspect of the Public School system and its problems has been the hold which it has exercised on the imagination of so many of the leading writers of the nineteenth and twentieth centuries. Rudyard Kipling (*Stalky & Co.*, 1899), F. A. Anstey (*Vice Versa*, 1902), Horace Annesley Vachell (*The Hill*, 1905), Sir Compton Mackenzie (*Sinister Street*, Vol. I, 1913), Ian Hay (*The Lighter Side of School Life*, 1914), Sir Shane Leslie (*The Oppidan*, 1922), Sir Hugh Walpole (*Jeremy at Crale*, 1927), P. G. Wodehouse (*Mike*, 1909 and the *Gold Bat*, 1904), and that strongly individualistic Old Malvernian Michael Arlen, less well-known by his original name of Dikran Koyoumdjian (*Piracy*, 1922), are among the more shining lights of the Public School story tellers. The reader can allow his taste to range between the reforming zeal of *Tom Brown's Schooldays* and the sheer entertainment value of *The Fifth Form at St. Dominic's*, and from the golden unreality of *David Blaize* to the picric analysis of *The Loom of Youth* and *Prelude*. The problems of the Public School system are represented with varying degrees of seriousness in all of these works and no man can consider himself fully briefed upon the subject who has not at least a passing familiarity with them.

Controversy over Public Schools will continue for many years, and there can be no attempt to give a final answer here. A study of their history, however, demonstrates a number of surprising features. For while the Public Schools have in the past claimed to be the leaders of our society, they have themselves been led by it ; and while they have been thought to be a privileged and separate section of the community, they have so often reflected its essential characteristics and trained their pupils to meet the particular needs of the day. This history will show Malvern College starting life under the influence of the Arnoldian ideal of the Christian gentlemen, reflecting later that of the growing power of the commercial community, and then, at the turn of the century, that of the empire-builders ; and subsequently sharing the revaluations that have been made and are still being made to meet the series of changes that have taken place in England and the rest of the world since the tragedy of 1914.

This relationship between the educational system and the needs of the present-day world is vital to a developing community. The assessment of the ideal rôle that a school like Malvern should play in contemporary society is not, and can never be, finally determined ; but it is clear that the objective at the present time should be to combine such of the ideas of earlier times as are of permanent value together with an academic training of the highest quality. First-hand observers of the scene at Malvern can recognize the size of the effort that is being made to do this ; the historian of the next hundred years will record how faithfully the ideals and activities of the school have prepared its members to be the citizens of the twenty-first century.

It is in this context that Mr. Ralph Blumenau has so admirably and felicitously written the history of the first hundred years of Malvern College. Not himself an Old Malvernian, Mr. Blumenau has brought to his task the dispassionate eye of the trained historian, but has also written with great warmth of understanding and sensitive appreciation. The result of his work is a book which, I confidently believe, no member of the School, past or present, can read without pride and no member of the general public without pleasure. As an Old Malvernian myself I am certainly proud to have been invited to contribute this foreword.

JOHN WHEELER-BENNETT

GARSINGTON MANOR
OXON.
May 1964

PREFACE

ANY historian of a school who, like the present author, has known it for only a very few years is particularly dependent on the help and good will of those who have long-standing connections and long memories ; and I have been fortunate indeed in the help on which I was able to draw in writing this book. In the first place, I would like to express my thanks to the College Council for having invited me to produce this history and in particular to the sub-committee which represented them while the book was being written and published : Sir John Wheeler-Bennett, General Sir Nevil Brownjohn and Ronald Maudsley, all Old Malvernians. They have given me help and encouragement from first to last, and I could not have had more benign taskmasters.

For the period after 1890 I was able to draw on the memories of men still alive. My greatest debt here is to the late R. B. Porch, who had been almost uninterruptedly connected with Malvern from 1888 onwards and was a mine of information about everything relating to the school. Sometimes he would send me pages and pages of reminiscences in his beautiful hand-writing and delightful English ; sometimes he would talk over the old days, puffing at his pipe the while. Always there was an old-world courtesy and charm about him which made it a real pleasure to consult him. His death in 1963 robbed many Malvernians of a dear friend and this History of still more material.

Sir Reginald Hills, also an indefatigable correspondent with a memory of school affairs stretching back to 1891, likewise gave up much of his time ; and so did R. T. Colthurst, whose extensive comments on my first draft were absolutely invaluable. Others who have made many helpful suggestions after having read the typescript are F. S. Preston, the Rev. H. C. A. Gaunt, D. D. Lindsay, and L. R. Dodd.

One of my pupils, L. M. Turner, spent much time digging

out references to the College from old numbers of the *Malvern Gazette* ; and several people whose connections with Malvern are remote and indirect have also supplied information. Above all, I am grateful to the many Old Malvernians who have written or talked to me, sometimes at considerable length, about their school days. I hope that they will not find too many sins of omission or commission in the pages that follow and that they will recognize the picture I have drawn of their School.

R. K. B.

CONTENTS

LIST OF ILLUSTRATIONS

CHAPTER I

Foundations, 1853 – 1865

THE middle of the nineteenth century saw a great expansion of the public school system. This was due in part to the growing prosperity and ambition of the middle classes, who were anxious that their sons should have the same education as the old ruling classes were having, though it is doubtful whether they would have sent their sons away to schools if the conditions within them had remained quite as barbaric as they were in the eighteenth and early nineteenth centuries. Brutality, licentiousness, and indiscipline had been widespread in the preceding period. Indeed, the old ruling classes themselves would not have put up with these conditions for much longer.

The work of a number of reforming headmasters — Russell at Charterhouse, Butler at Shrewsbury, and of course Arnold at Rugby — came therefore at just the right time. Their work is too well known to be described here. The fact is that they saved the public schools as important institutions, restored to them respectability and prestige, and paved the way for an enormous increase in public school education. In the 1840s, 1850s, and 1860s a large number of new schools was founded ; and the coming of the railway during these decades also made it easier for parents to send their boys away from home.

The new schools were financed in a variety of ways. Sometimes the money was put up by private subscription, as for instance in the case of the Woodard Schools. The money for Wellington College was raised by public subscription to a memorial to the Duke of Wellington. Some schools were started by proprietary companies and financed by the sale of shares. Of this last group Cheltenham College, founded in 1841, was a good and successful example. By 1861 it had 600 boys on its books and its shares, originally issued at £20, had risen to £120. The school brought new prosperity to a town whose reputation as a spa was passing away at that time.

What had happened in Cheltenham could hardly go un-noticed in nearby Malvern. Here, too, the town had come to invest heavily in the water cure. Taking the Malvern waters had become fashionable after the publication in 1757 of Dr John Wall's *Experiments and Observations on the Malvern Waters*. His commendation of their purity gave rise to the couplet

> The Malvern water, says Dr. Wall,
> Is famed for containing just nothing at all ;

and in fact it is now thought to be the purest natural water in the world.[1]

The centre of the cure was originally Malvern Wells ; but by about 1780 the more important visitors stayed at Great Malvern and drove or walked over to the Wells. A royal visit by the Duchess of Kent and the Princess Victoria in 1831 set the seal of fame on the spa ; and the quiet little village nestling under the hills, which in 1801 had a population of only 819, became a bustling Victorian resort whose population reached 2,768 in 1841. Then, in 1842, Dr James Wilson and his partner Dr James Gully arrived in Malvern. Wilson had learnt 'hydropathy' in Germany, and the two men introduced this form of the water cure into Malvern. Their success was phenomenal : Wilson treated 350 patients in four months during his first year ; and Gully had a way with the great that brought him such distinguished patients as Carlyle, Macaulay, Tennyson, and Gladstone. Wilson and Gully parted soon after 1846 and became rivals. Other competitors were soon in the field. The railway, which reached Malvern in 1859, brought about 3,000 visitors a year to the town ; and the cost of land quadrupled in twenty years.[2]

It was at this time that the project for building a college

in Malvern was first mooted. The originator of the idea was Walter Burrow. He had come to live in Malvern at the end of 1849 as manager of a branch of Messrs. Lea & Perrins of Worcester, whom he describes in a memorandum as 'the well-known Chemists of that city' and in whose dispensary the formula for Lea & Perrins Worcester Sauce was developed. On these foundations the Lea and Perrins families built up a very considerable fortune, and we shall later find their members figuring prominently among the benefactors of Malvern College. They took Walter Burrow and his brother John into partnership soon after the latters' arrival in Malvern ; and when the senior partners retired, the Burrow brothers bought their shares in the Malvern business and carried it on themselves. They began to bottle the water from St. Ann's Well ; eventually became the sole lessees of the spring ; and won gold medal after gold medal at international exhibitions for the purity of their 'Alpha Brand' Malvern Water which, in its brown glass-stoppered bottles, was sent all over Britain and indeed further afield.[3]

Walter Burrow writes : 'We found Malvern a rather quiet place, though it was developing life through the introduction of the then very fashionable "Water Cure", just inaugurated by Drs Wilson and Gully. Looking ahead, we saw the probability of a considerable advance in the prosperity of the Town, and determined to do our utmost to promote it. Many methods were discussed and, among others, the lighting of the Town with Gas was brought about by our initiative.' He thought much about the example of Cheltenham College, and in 1853 'came to the conclusion that what had proved possible at Cheltenham might be equally possible at Malvern, which in many respects had, I considered, advantages superior to those of Cheltenham for such an institution'.

They had another brother, the Rev. H. H. Burrow, then at Oxford ; and he sought the advice of some heads of colleges, notably of the Warden of New College, Dr. Sewell, on how to proceed. They then brought in the Rev. Frank Dyson of

Malvern, and he in turn secured the cooperation of the Hon. Frederick Lygon. Lygon, a son of the local magnate, the fourth Earl Beauchamp, was a Member of Parliament and a man of very considerable wealth. He was later to become a member of Disraeli's Government in 1874 and of Salisbury's in 1885 and 1886. He was a High Anglican and one of the founders of Keble College, Oxford. When he agreed to become Chairman of the College Council, it was easy to form a strong committee of local notables : Lord Lyttelton, who was related to Gladstone and was Lord Lieutenant of Worcestershire ; Sir Edmund Lechmere, Bt., M.P.; 'that Napoleon of hydropathy', Dr Gully ; 4 Canon Melville of Worcester Cathedral, who had been headmaster of Radley College ; John Wheeley Lea, a partner in Lea & Perrins ; and many others. The Burrow brothers, for all the hard work they had done, never figured on the Council : one suspects they were not considered to be socially sufficiently eminent ; and when Walter Burrow died in 1913, his part in the history of the College seems to have been so completely forgotten that the school was not even represented at his funeral.* His part would not be known today were it not for a bundle of his manuscript papers which John Burrow's granddaughter sent to the Headmaster in 1960, thinking that they might be of interest to the College.

In the winter of 1857/8 there was a financial crash which brought down half the banks of England, and the floating of new educational concerns had to be postponed for some time. It took another four years before the Committee decided to proceed, as had Cheltenham College, by forming a proprietary company, which Lea was prepared to guarantee to the extent of £10,000. Before the Company was officially constituted, they looked for a site and had some difficulty in finding what

---

* Among the mourners, however, was F. M. Prosser, the first School Porter, who had retired in 1906. (*Malvern Gazette*, January 17, 1913.) C. W. Dyson Perrins was present at John Burrow's funeral three years later, but probably in a private capacity rather than as a representative of the College.

they wanted until Dr Leopold Stummes, a German-born hydropath who was the Secretary of the Committee, secured fourteen acres, which are the nucleus of the present grounds.* It was a site whose slope was to present some expensive problems, but it could scarcely be more beautiful, with the hills rising steeply above it and with a sweeping view over the green valley below, checked by Dripshill and Bredon but limited only by the Cotswolds on the horizon.

The Rev. H. H. Burrow was entrusted with drawing up the first prospectus ; and its wording shows the change that was beginning to come over the curriculum of a public school education. True, Classics was still saluted as the queen of studies :

'Classical literature will necessarily occupy a prominent place in the prescribed course of study, for over and above its intrinsic worth as a storehouse of positive knowledge, it affords the best groundwork for subsequent advance in the study of modern languages ; added to this advantage, Greek and Latin authors furnish the truest principle of taste in composition ; they give an insight into the policy and character of men and manners in different stages of society, and by the patient study which they demand, discipline the mind and prepare it for the acquirement of information on all other subjects.' Mathematics would receive the recognition due to that important branch of study ; and then, reflecting the controversy which was at that time raging about the narrowness of the curriculum at some of the older public schools,[5] the prospectus continues : 'Especial regard will also be paid to those elements which are daily rising in importance, but which as yet have hardly been admitted as matters of systematic teaching. The fact that valuable civil and military appointments are now thrown open for general competition,† forces

---

* Stummes became Wilson's partner at about this time (Brian S. Smith, *History of Malvern*, Chapter XI). Since Wilson and Gully had by then become irreconcilable rivals (*ibid.*), Stummes must have been something of a diplomat to be able to work with both men.

† Army and Civil Service examinations had been introduced in 1855.

upon our notice the necessity of making the study of Physical Science, Modern History, and Languages, not merely a casual but an admitted and regular pursuit.'

At last everything was ready for the formal foundation of the Company, and this took place on August 22, 1862, in Dr Gully's Dining Room at the Imperial Hotel (which he had built for the accommodation of his patients and which is today occupied by Malvern Girls' College). There it was formally resolved, 'That a Proprietary College, to be established in an eligible situation, as nearly as possible on the model of the Public Schools for the Education of the Sons of Gentlemen, at a moderate cost, is an undertaking highly desirable in the present state of education in England, and, if well-conducted, likely to be successful and of great public benefit.'

'That the town of Malvern, from its bracing air, gravelly soil, pure water, and convenient access by Railway, is well adapted for an undertaking of this nature.'

'That the Prospectus for founding at Malvern a Proprietary College Company, limited, now read, be approved.'

'That the Prospectus with the foregoing resolutions be inserted in the Worcester and Malvern papers.'*

The Council also advertised for an architect and for a headmaster. Forty designs were submitted under pseudonyms. 'Labor Omnia Vincit' was the pseudonym used by the successful competitor, Charles Hansom, brother of the inventor of the Hansom cab. He had already built Clifton College with a very similar layout and in that same neo-Gothic style which was supposed to convey both the Christian nature of the education provided within its walls and the atmosphere of Oxford and Cambridge, for which the public schools were a preparation.[6] Walter Burrow had had in mind a school of 600 boys, of the same size, that is, as Cheltenham, and the main building was intended to accommodate something like

---

* Later that year the Council also advertised in the national Press : *The Times*, the *Daily News*, the *Morning Post*, the *Illustrated London News*, the *Saturday Review*, and the local papers in Worcester, Birmingham, Liverpool, Manchester, Bristol, Cheltenham, and Leeds.

that number. In the true Victorian manner, the class-room windows were placed so high that boys could not be distracted by what was going on outside. But we must probably blame a desire to make the most economical use of space for the fact that the sunny view towards the east was allocated to the corridors, whilst the class-rooms for the most part faced either north or towards the Hills which rise so steeply behind the College that one of the masters retiring in 1889 was able to say that some of his happiest hours had been spent in a form room into which a ray of sunlight had never gleamed during the fifteen years he had taught there.[7]

The Foundation Stone was laid by the Bishop of Worcester on July 22, 1863. Four hundred invitations had been sent out, and each guest was presented with 'a steel engraving of the College, beautifully executed and suitable for a frame or the album'.[8] There were the toasts and speeches usual on such occasions; but Dr Gully, replying to the toast 'The Prosperity of Malvern', introduced a somewhat jarring note by berating the townspeople for having taken up only twelve of the five hundred shares. 'They knew, he said, how tribes of medical and other professional men had come into the town and thriven. He could not understand how it was that the townspeople would not look beyond their noses, for with five hundred students there, there must be an increased expenditure of something like £100,000 per annum in Malvern.'[9] It was not the most auspicious start to good relations between the townsfolk and the College; and three years after the College had opened, it was for the town to ventilate a grievance. The *Malvern News* then wrote, 'One regret we may be permitted to express; that a body of intelligent gentlemen such as compose the teaching staff of the College do not take more part in the lectures, and other devices of the locality, to increase the amount of intelligence to be diffused by those means among the trading community of the town. These are not the days for the formation of close social corporations living to themselves and for themselves, like those products of the twilight of civilization, the inhabitants of that portion of the cathedral towns so appropriately named the Close. Clever philologists, acute mathematicians, surely do not aim to imitate such drowsy mortals as those !' [10]

Once the Foundation Stone had been laid, work went on apace. On May 12, 1864, to the pealing of bells and the music of a Rifle Volunteers Band, a hundred and eighty workmen walked in procession to the Belle Vue Hotel for the traditional gargantuan rearing supper to celebrate the laying of the roof-timbers. After working their way through 'fish, roast and boiled mutton, fillets of veal, lamb, hams, and pigeon pies, &c, &c, with plum puddings and pastry', the men had to listen to the speeches appropriate to the occasion and to the following reflections from the Vicar : 'The rev. gentleman warmly counselled the cultivation of friendly feelings among the operative portion of the community, and eulogized honest, noble, high principled labour. The evil influence of strikes was pointed out, and the notion that the interests of employers and employed were antagonistic combated as a grand delusion.' [11] These sentiments were prompted by a strike, lasting about a week, which had taken place locally in the building trade in the previous month. More serious delay was caused later by the difficulty in getting building materials. It had been hoped to open the College in September 1864 — only fourteen months after the Foundation Stone had been laid — but the work took three months longer than had been anticipated. At one stage the Council threatened the con-tractors, Messrs. Warburton Bros. of Manchester, with legal action if the work was not completed in time for the opening ; and when the day came, there were many last touches still to be added to the main building. The College Chapel, which Hansom had designed to stand where the present chapel stands and to be connected with the Main Building by a covered passage, had not even been begun, and financial difficulties prevented its erection for many years. In the meantime that part of the South Wing which today houses the Upper and

Lower Grundy Libraries and the three class-rooms under-neath the Upper Grundy* was used as a Chapel and was indeed quite suitable for that function as long as the school remained small in numbers.

The choice of Warburton's as the contractors was a very unhappy one. It is difficult at this distance of time to tell whether they were driven into irresponsibly bad building by having underestimated the time needed for completion, or whether they were just bad builders. In any case, within a year the north corridor showed settlements and was con-sidered so unsafe that props had to be put up against the out-side wall; rain came through the roof of the Chapel and of one of the class-rooms; a ceiling in School House fell in; and the first two boarding-houses, which were also built by Warburton's, had no dry courses surrounding the basement, and this necessitated very expensive repairs within three years. Understandably, Hansom refused the contractors the final certificate; the Council withheld payment; the matter had to be taken to court; and in the end it was settled on a com-promise basis by arbitration.

The cost of the repair to the two boarding-houses was not borne by the College Council, for they were not its property. The original share capital of the College was only £20,000 in 500 shares of £40 each. On the day the school opened, 476 of the 500 shares had been taken up; and the rest were taken up by March 1867, when a further 100 shares were issued, to increase the share capital to £24,000. Obviously such a sum was quite inadequate to finance the building of boarding-houses as well as of the main College Building. In October 1863 the College Council sold half an acre of land to Lygon on which he then built a house for the residence of the Head-master, who was to pay him £200 a year in rent. This was the beginning of School House. But for building boarding-houses, sixteen of the most prominent of the shareholders

---

* There was then no partition between the three class-rooms nor a ceiling between them and the Upper Grundy.

(many of them on the College Council) formed themselves into a separate Company, called the Building Company, with a share capital of £15,000 in 150 shares of £100 each. The new Building Company then bought from the College Company an acre of land and gave the contract for designing two houses (the present Nos. 1 and 2) to Hansom and for building them to Warburton. These houses were then leased to the College at a rent which would give the Building Company's shareholders a six per cent return on their investment. The College was to have the right to buy the property of the Building Company within ten years. In fact it was to take thirteen years before the College was financially strong enough to raise the mortgages for this operation. It would not have been able to do so even then if it had not been for the generosity which the Building Company showed to the College during a time which was financially extremely critical. The school could not have survived that period if the Company had insisted on regular and full payment of interest. Two men who sustained great financial loss in the interests of the College were Lygon, who succeeded his brother as the sixth Earl Beauchamp in 1866, and John Wheeley Lea, for they were the biggest of the shareholders of the Building Company ; and it is no exaggeration to think of these two men as the principal founding benefactors of Malvern College.

CHAPTER II

The Headmastership of Arthur Faber
1865–1880

THE advertisement for the Headmastership brought twenty-five applicants ; and on the recommendation of the Bishop of Worcester the Council appointed on March 30, 1863, the thirty-two-year-old Reverend Arthur Faber, a Wykehamist and Fellow and Tutor of New College, Oxford. His portrait shows a firm but humorous character, a sensitive and generous mouth, eyes with a sense of fun : one feels that he must have understood the young, and indeed he was 'just the subject to arouse hero-worship in boys'.[1] He received a handsome salary : £800 a year plus an additional £200 until the number of boys in the school should have reached 400 (which it never did in his time) and a capitation fee of £3 for every boy after the first 200.* The Council accepted Faber's recommendations for the number and salary of the assistant masters. The senior classical and mathematical masters were to receive £250 a year. In case this figure were thought too low, Faber pointed out that these two men would be the housemasters of the two new houses which were expected to provide an extra income even after the rental of £300 had been paid. The next two masters were to have £200 with a promise of the next two houses which, if the school did even moderately well, were certain to be required within a very short time. There was also to be on the teaching staff a Frenchman and a German teaching part-time. The men appointed during the first three years were all, with the exception of the foreign masters, in Holy Orders. As for the

---

* The school reached this number in 1875.

headmaster, he was required to be in priest's orders by the Constitution of the College.

On January 25, 1865, the College officially opened with twenty-four boys of whom eleven were day boys (or 'home-boarders', as they were called) and six assistant masters. Only one of the two boarding-houses was ready, and the boys in No. 2 spent that first term in Holyrood House (now part of the Tudor Hotel) and moved into their new quarters on the last day but one of the first term. During the night before the College opened, there had been an exceptionally heavy fall of snow, and the very first thing the boys in No. 1 had to do was to dig a way up to the College with improvised spades.

The tuition fees were £25 per annum; the boarding fees, which were paid to the housemasters, £60 per annum. Running a house was a completely private enterprise at Malvern, as it was at most public schools at that time. A house that was full would bring in a handsome profit to the housemaster; but in the early years numbers rose slowly, and the first housemasters frequently asked the Council to remit part of their rent of £300 a year — a request which was almost invariably refused. Not until No. 5 was opened in 1871 did the Council take into account the early financial difficulties which were bound to face any housemaster until his house was full. By the new arrangement, a rent of £5 per boy was paid until the numbers exceeded twenty, £7 until they exceeded thirty, and thereafter the full rent of £300 was due. There were other charges on the housemasters. Until 1870 they were required to pay 6/8 per boy per term towards a seat in the Chapel; they also supplied the beds for the sanatorium and paid part of the wages of its staff. The Sanatorium at this time was housed in what is today the Art School on the first floor of the South Wing, and initially a 'Charwoman and Nurse' was appointed to look after it, at £18 a year.

When the school opened, the curriculum taught to the

three forms into which the boys were divided consisted of Classics, Mathematics, French, German, and Music. In 1867 Faber added the Modern Department, in which English Literature, Modern History, and Composition were taught. Chemistry lessons were given outside the curriculum and until 1887 at an additional cost ; but there is no indication that any boy availed himself of the other optional subjects which one of the early prospectuses offered for an extra charge. Since these included the Sanskrit, Hindustani, and Persian languages, that is perhaps not very surprising.

From 1870 onwards the school began to display its academic prowess in public in a variety of ways. The College began to be examined by outside examiners in that year. Extracts from Greek, Latin, English, and French plays were performed on Speech Day, and these were always preceded by a witty Prologue in English verse (composed in later years chiefly by H. W. Smith) which was full of allusions to the events of the year. 1870 also saw the first university awards at Oxford and Cambridge. But there was some doubt whether Malvern attracted enough boys with academic ambitions. The reduction of fees for the sons of clergymen in 1870 was justified on the grounds that 'it is necessary for the efficiency of the upper part of the School, that there should be adequate Competition amongst the Scholars ; but as many of the pupils have been destined for Mercantile pursuits, they have left without reaching the highest forms, thus rendering it difficult to maintain so active a competition as is desirable. It has therefore been thought right to take measures to attract to the College a larger number of pupils destined for the Universities.' [2] After 1872 there was never a year without university awards. In a moderately good year there would be five or six ; in a few exceptionally good years there were nine or ten. This was not bad, especially when, as the first issue of the *Malvern Register* in 1894 felt constrained to point out, 'It must always be remembered, in judging of the intellectual distinctions of a School like Malvern, that it has few attractions in the way of scholarships to offer to clever boys, as compared with the rich foundations of the older Public Schools'.[3]

The successes that were achieved were due to Faber's thorough and ruthless teaching. False quantities and concords were punished with fifty lines of Virgil for each mistake. When the boys wanted a half-holiday to play a match, the senior prefect could petition the Headmaster ; but the petition had to be written in impeccable Latin, explaining the reason for the request and the manner in which it was proposed to spend the holiday. An O.M. recalled in 1910 : 'It fell to my lot to have to elaborate many such letters, and a difficult job it was to express in decent Latin such terms as football, fives, cricket, and so on. On one occasion I made a false concord and the half was refused, to my extreme confusion and the wrath of the school.' For class-room translation into Latin and Greek, Faber produced his own elegant versions which, after the boys had produced their own inelegant ones, had to be written out as fair copies.

He was a strict disciplinarian and insisted absolutely on punctuality and on work being handed in on time. 'Did you go to bed last night ?' was his reply to the boy who pleaded that he had had to play in a match the day before and so could not get the work done.

But he disliked caning as a punishment and saw to it that his staff kept it down to a minimum. In 1868 he recorded in his diary the instruction 'that no caning should be inflicted before a communication to himself giving the name of [the] boy and the nature of the offence. The punishment to take place across the shoulders, and without stripping of the jacket.' He had been sincere when he declared in the speech he had made on the occasion of the laying of the Foundation Stone that he would select for his staff 'men who would not only be masters, but who would stand in the relation to the pupils of senior friend and junior friend. There must be mutual confidence between all parties. There must be that *entente cordiale* without which no infant school could grow out of its swaddling clothes.' ⁴ So it was characteristic of him that he should rattle his bunch of keys loudly as he strode down the corridor to his class-room, to give warning of his approach ; and underneath his strictness he had a kindly sense of humour, so that he compelled affection as well as respect from those he drove so hard.

Besides, it was no harder than he drove himself. He was a phenomenally swift and methodical worker who packed an enormous amount of activity into every day. The school's working day began at seven o'clock with an hour's work before breakfast — a feature of school life modelled on Winchester, though with the modification that Wykehamists used to begin the day in summer at six o'clock ; and Faber used to go for a good walk before seven o'clock school. In the winter, it was only the Headmaster's forms, the Sixth and Fifth, whose presence was required at this unearthly hour. Other masters and their forms were spared the ordeal, and in the later years of Faber's headmastership even his forms were let off early-morning school between mid-November and mid-February. It was not until Grundy's time that school before breakfast was suspended throughout the Christmas and Easter terms and not until Gaunt's days that it was abolished in the summer.

After early-morning school, there was a hearty breakfast : there was unlimited bread and butter, and the house butler would cook any eggs, bacon, or kidneys the boys had bought and handed in to him. After breakfast came morning school until twelve o'clock. It was interrupted by a break, in which of course there was a rush to 'Buggy's Bower' (Bowket's sweetshop) at the rear of the rickety structure that served as a pavilion. 'He kept a very good assortment of cakes and sweets', reminisced an O.M. in 1925. 'The chief one I can remember was his celebrated fourpenny buster ; it was an immense muffin cut in two and generously sandwiched with slices of ham. There was also a small addition like a ticket office annexed, where every morning a boy, in terror of his life, was shut in, selling hot rolls for breakfast. It was the fashion to "hot" for rolls when we came out of early school, and the edifice used to threaten to collapse. One celebrated morning as we came out of school, to our delight "Buggy's" roll boy was late and we saw him coming up the grounds with his basket. There was a yell of joy ; the unfortunate youth roughly calculated if he could make the hut in time, decided he couldn't : so he dropped the basket and ran for his life. The wolves stopped for the basket and rolls, so his life was spared.' Relations between the College Boys (the Lads) and the boys from the town (the Cads) were never friendly and there was many a battle between them under the big Spanish chestnut tree in the Firs.

But to revert to the daily routine : there was an hour for games between the end of morning school and the mid-day dinner — this last a generous repast washed down with plenty of beer. Afternoon school was from 3 to 5.30 ; tea at 6 ; preparation from 7 to 8 ; supper at 8.30 ; and evening prayers at 8.45. 'Boys were always expected to say their prayers night and morning and I believe everyone did, and anyone neglecting to do this was jumped on by the others', a young O.M. wrote in his diary soon after leaving school in the 1870s.

On one of the two half-holidays there was 'impot. school' — impositions consisting in those days, not of essays or work to be done again, but of passages or sentences having to be copied out in a fair hand. A legible and even beautiful hand was far more rigidly insisted on in those days than it is today, as almost every document that has furnished material for this period bears witness. Imposition paper had to be bought at the cost of a penny a sheet from Prosser, the School Porter, a splendid character who for thirty-six years commented shrewdly and inimitably on the life of the school. With a later generation of boys he was reputed to have applied for the post of public hangman before he came to Malvern.

Such then was the routine of daily life which was established in the early days of the College. Within five years of its opening, the school numbered 190, and 'Veteranus' in the first number of the *Malvernian* (which appeared in 1869) could look back over those first five years as if they were an age. The boys seem to have been somewhat unruly when they first came. Faber did not initially believe in the Prefects' System as it had been transformed by Arnold. Here, too, he at first modelled Malvern on Winchester, where Moberly, headmaster from 1835 to 1866, had failed to bring the prefect system under his control. Winchester prefects for many years retained their traditional independence and 'the morality that the boys imbibed continued to be the result of rigid custom among the boys, not of master influence'.[5] Faber at first accepted this system and used to say, before experience taught him otherwise, that if boys were left to tumble about on their heads, they would teach themselves to stand on their feet. But in a new school this worked less well than in one which had five centuries of tradition behind it (and even there it could scarcely be said to be a good system). During the school's first year, for instance, the small boys in No. 1 were absolutely terrorized by two venomous bullies; and one of the victims arrived home so ill that his parents protested and the older bully was expelled. Faber came to see the need for a more controlled authority in the houses, and by 1868 a prefectorial system on Arnold's lines had been introduced. It needed a little time to work smoothly, since everything had to be done for the first time; and the constant arrival of newcomers, who each year outnumbered those who were already at the school and who included a fair sprinkling of boys of fifteen, sixteen or even seventeen, cannot have made the creation of a tradition of discipline very easy. 'Veteranus' comments, 'The great want of that time (a want which, we are afraid, is *scarcely even now fully supplied*) was a unanimous coalition of the seniors of the school on the side of order and authority.' However, he was clearly satisfied with the progress that had been made since then: rules had been drawn up, the prefectorial system was working well, fagging had been

the subject of games and of the many little ways in which the boys thought that the conditions under which they lived could be improved. There was a column for correspondence, the vast majority of which concerned itself with games, the exchange of letters between 'Ritualist' and 'Non-Ritualist' about the wearing of surplices in Chapel being one of the extremely rare irruptions of a non-athletic character.

A feature which affected games at Malvern in the early years was the extraordinary slope of the playing fields. It will be remembered that the site on which the College was built had been acquired for the school by Dr Stummes, the original Secretary of the Council. 'But Dr Stummes knew probably little of cricket or other school games, nor does their importance seem to have had due weight with those who first combined to create and launch into the world this School of ours', wrote the Rev. Henry Foster, the moving spirit behind games at Malvern from 1867 to 1915. 'When it first opened in the month of February [*sic*] 1865, there was but little to justify the hope of future athletic greatness. Not a level spot anywhere ; not a court, not a shed, only a broad sweep of turf tilted uniformly in one direction, with a slope of 1 in 15, and, worse than all, no money to do anything with.' [6] And Faber wrote, 'No imagination can conceive of this field as other than unhappily narrow and circumscribed. Being thus limited in dimension, nature had also chosen to lay it down at an acute angle. It was not that it sloped here and there, but that it sloped everywhere. Therefore no wise man contended that, for the purposes of pure cricket, it was beyond criticism. Nevertheless, like many other unpromising things, it proved better than its promise. It had its defects, but it had its compensations also. It soon turned out that the natives had an advantage over the outsiders, though the level sward of present times was not then general ; * still, a slope quite as

---

* Faber knew what he was talking about. He had been an excellent cricketer, though after his ordination he had, as was the custom of those days, to play under a pseudonym. 'When Mr "St. Fabian" made three

evident as ours was rare. If the enemy was beaten, he had something to remark about the pitch. I think we mostly won our matches : no doubt we did not search for the strongest enemy we could find. But an enemy retiring in defeat sometimes so forgot the far conventions of fine breeding as to murmur something about playing on the roof of a house. But no one was troubled by these murmurs. A generous victor will allow his enemy to say anything.'

The College was certainly more than anxious to forgo such unfair advantages as nature provided. A meeting of the Headmaster, the games masters, and the Cricket Eleven passed a resolution 'to the effect that a level pitch was necessary to the due development of cricket', and in 1872 the Senior Turf was levelled. The expenses of this and other levelling operations came to £1,200, provided mainly by debentures taken up by masters and their friends. Malvern could now offer respectable hospitality to Repton and to Shrewsbury, whom it had begun to play in 1871.

Of the next eighteen matches against Repton, Malvern won only two ; and the levelling of the cricket pitch did not produce better cricketers. '*L'homme propose, Dieu dispose,*' sighed the Rev. Foster piously. Faber discussed the matter from a less philosophical point of view : 'It was really a pretty question whether the acute angle (of the cricket pitch) helped to make a future bowler or to mar him. Did it suggest to him, by what actually took place, the advantage of a sharp break, and so incline him to obtain by his own exertion a similar break on more level pitches ? Or did it satisfy him too soon by what it gratuitously offered him, and so incline him to rest on his oars before the boat had gone under weigh ? *Utrum horum ?*' He left the question open, though in a reminiscence from an Old Boy we find it categorically stated that 'bowlers had an easy time of it then, "they toiled not

figures at Lord's for Harlequins *v*. Quidnuncs, it was a fairly open secret who the crack hitter was. In those times Lord's was no billiard table.' (*The Field*, December 3, 1910.) The pitch at Lord's was both rough and on a slope. Like James later, Faber never wore pads.

THE SCHOOL FOOTBALL XI, 1878

neither did they spin".'.[7] The fact is that the quality of Malvern cricket languished until the arrival of Charles Toppin in 1885 turned the scales.

Football, at Faber's wish, was first played at Malvern in its Winchester form. He and Foster (also an Old Wykehamist) often played on opposite sides and sent the ball soaring with huge kicks from one to the other over the heads of the opposing teams, perhaps half a dozen times in succession. When masters were not present, it was a pretty rough game, and even in house matches there were no referees. These house matches were most fiercely fought, and an O.M. of No. 1 recalled in the *Malvernian* sixty years later how even his housemaster, the Rev. McDowall, normally the most dignified of men with the appearance of a Landseer bloodhound wearing Dundreary whiskers, was stirred in the first match between his house and Drew's (No. 2) : 'Feeling was running very high—there were only a few minutes left for time and neither team had any material advantage, when Mr McDowall jumped up, waving his hat and shouted, "Go it, my boys, Sausages for tea !" The effect was magical. With the war-cry "Sausages and Doodles" we simply wiped the floor with "old Franky's" team (there were no referees then) and won a goal.' The efficacy of this type of war-cry is proved by the fact that, as we shall see later, it was still in use thirty years afterwards.

The Winchester form of football did not take root, and in 1873 it was another Old Wykehamist on the Malvern staff, the Rev. A. W. H. Howard, who committed the school to Association football. Impossible for a Wykehamist to introduce Rugby football : for whilst Winchester was the model which schools of High Church leanings claimed to imitate, Arnold's Rugby served as the acknowledged pattern for schools of an Evangelical inspiration. The three Wykehamist clergy on the Malvern staff reluctantly abandoned Winchester football ; but to have adopted Rugby football in its place would have been not only disloyal to their old school, but theologically suspect into the bargain.[8]

THE REV. A. FABER, HEADMASTER 1865 to 1880

and then the players have to fetch it, which if there were plenty of kickers-in might be prevented and a great deal of time saved. We all know that it is not pleasant having to stand about upon a cold day, but every junior must take his chance, and if they want to warm themselves, they must move about their beat.' From another letter it appears that boys who had been taken off games by the school doctor were often dragooned into kicking-in.

The juniors had a respite in the period between the cricket and the football seasons. It was several times suggested in the *Malvernian* that Hockey might be played during that period, and one such letter discusses the objection that Hockey is a '*caddish* game' : 'But why in the world should this objection be raised ? Do not all ranks join in football and cricket ? Nay, we are even taught by professional men who belong to the lower classes ; and in these games gentleman meets rustic, and nobleman meets snob on terms of perfect equality.'

The tone of this may make a modern reader wince or smile, according to temperament. The feeling of superiority to the lower classes was more openly expressed in those days than it is today ; and the Council minutes of those years omit the prefix of Mr before the names of College servants and tradesmen. But the boys were made aware of their social responsibilities by the College Mission. In 1878, on Foster's initiative, the Patteson Society was founded, named after a missionary bishop in the Melanesian Islands. Its original object was to help foreign missions ; but after only a very short time, it found work nearer home and in 1882 adopted the Parish of All Saints, Haggerston, in the East End of London, and contributed £80 a year towards providing a parish nurse. What grew out of these small beginnings will be found in later chapters.

It is time now to trace the growth of the College during Faber's headmastership. It will be remembered that the first two houses had been opened together with the College in 1865, No. 1 under the Rev. Charles McDowall, later to be headmaster of Highgate, and No. 2 under the Rev. F. R. Drew. In 1865 the Building Company bought Radnor Field * on which to build the South Houses. These, needless to say, were not constructed by Messrs. Warburton ; but neither was Hansom the architect. He had not been able to come to Malvern often enough during the time of the subsidence troubles and the Council had refused to pay his bills in full as a result. The designing of Nos. 3 and 4 was entrusted to Mr Hopkins of Worcester. No. 3 was opened in 1867 under the Rev. W. H. Maddock and No. 4 in the following year under the Rev. L. Estridge. The last house built under Faber's headmastership was No. 5 in 1871, designed by the architectural firm of Haddon Bros. The name No. 5 was originally given to the house which since 1908 has been known as No. 6.† Its first housemaster was the Rev. Henry Foster, who, as we have already seen, was the driving force behind a great deal of what was going on at Malvern in those days. He and his seven sons (of whom more anon) were superb Rackets players ; so it is fitting that a Rackets Court should have been built next door to his House in 1881. He also was the organizer of the construction of the Swimming Baths in 1892 ; in 1883, at the request of the boys, he started the Artillery Cadet Corps, the forerunner of today's Combined Cadet Force ; and he was originally in charge of the music as well.

All the new houses were built by the Building Company whose few shareholders had doubled their investment in 1866 by raising the share capital to £30,000 ; and the College owed, as has been said before, a rent of six per cent of the value of the property. Such debts could have been honoured only if the school had been as full as the founders had expected it to be. But though the numbers rose steadily during Faber's headmastership and reached 275 at one point, this was still far short of what the example of Cheltenham

---

* From the Trustees of E. T. Foley, for £4,300.
† See p. 71 below.

had led one to think could be achieved at Malvern. Part of
the trouble was that Malvern, unlike Cheltenham or Clifton,
was not sufficiently near a large town to be able to make up
the early shortage of boarders with day boys. Another
difficulty was that the shareholders did not nominate enough
boys. Each of the 500 shares of the College gave its owner
the right to nominate one boy. Any boy so nominated had
£6 deducted from his fees. If a shareholder omitted to
nominate a pupil, the place could be filled by the Council,
which would, however, pay £6 of the fees to the shareholder.
If every shareholder had nominated a boy for each share, the
school would soon have been full, and the sanguine expecta-
tions of the promoters would have been fulfilled. Unfortunately, very few of the shareholders were able to make
nominations — Earl Beauchamp, for example, who held
twenty-five shares, could not possibly have nominated twenty-
five boys — and considerable advertising by the Council did
not bring in enough applications to fill the vacancies.

Under those circumstances, the debt to the Building Company weighed extremely heavily on the College. Only once,
in 1866, did it pay a large part of its debt in cash. After that
it was compelled to pay in interest-bearing debentures, and
even that proved a heavy burden. In 1871 matters had reached
a desperate point ; and it was then that the few individuals
who made up the Building Company made the generous
sacrifice alluded to earlier. In 1873 the College was able to
show for the first time in its history an excess of income over
expenditure ; and in 1876 it decided to raise money to buy
up all the assets of the Building Company — the five houses,
twenty-five acres of land and the Fives Court which had been
built ★ in 1867 — all for £45,000. The Building Company,
having done great service to the College, now ceased to exist.

School House of course remained the property of Earl
Beauchamp ; and it had a rather chequered early history. In
1871 Maddock left No. 3, and it was decided at that time that

★ In the Winchester style, of course : not the Eton or Rugby style.

it would be a good thing for the Headmaster to run a House. Faber therefore took over No. 3, which for a few years became known as School House, while the house formerly called by that name became a home for the bachelor masters on the staff. The expansion of the school, however, made the opening of another house desirable ; and in 1876 the bachelor masters had to find other accommodation, as the Rev. Howard began to turn their house into a sixth boarding-house. Ill health forced him to leave later that year, and in 1877 Faber handed No. 3 under its old name over to the Rev. T. Spear and moved back into the old School House as housemaster. The headmaster was to be housemaster of School House until the Second World War.

In 1880 Faber retired from the Headmastership, to become Rector of Sprotborough, Doncaster, and eventually a Canon of York. Toppin wrote in 1915, 'His character dominated his surroundings to such an extent that the School was colloquially known as "Faber's School" '.[9] Toppin claimed that 'he gave to Malvern a Wykehamist character which it has never wholly lost'. That Faber hoped to do this there is little doubt, if one can go by such small items of evidence as early morning school, his reluctance to introduce the Rugby-style prefect system, his desire to have football and Fives played according to the Winchester rules, and his introduction of the Winchester 'Dulce Domum' as the song which was sung by the school at the end of term. Like the football, the Domum had some difficulty in finding favour at Malvern. Five years after its introduction, the first issue of the *Malvernian* comments that this 'time-honoured song might yet, we think, *be sung with greater effect and vigour* than hereto' ; but it was sung with increasing lustiness as the years went by and the number of voices grew. Certainly Faber wanted to bring to Malvern Wykehamist characteristics less trifling than football rules or school songs. It would be interesting to know what precisely these were and in what way they were still in evidence when Toppin wrote ; but, alas, no records survive which would enable a historian to speak of this with confidence.

In any case, Malvern was fortunate in its first headmaster, in recognition of which fact he was elected onto the College Council, whilst his friends raised £400 to found an Exhibition in his name.* During his time the College had come through very severe financial difficulties. Faber had undoubtedly imprinted on it the character of a public school and, though numbers had risen more slowly than had been expected when the College was founded, the school seemed set for continuing progress and expansion on his retirement. The sharp setback it suffered during the next few years could hardly have been anticipated.

* A later generation commemorated him with the Faber Gate at the top of Woodshears Road (1915) and with a window in the Chapel (1921).

CHAPTER III

The Headmastership of C. T. Cruttwell
1880–1885

AS Faber's successor the Council elected the Rev. C. T. Cruttwell, a Fellow and former Tutor of Merton College and a former headmaster of Bradfield College.★ He was a scholar who had already published a standard History of Roman Literature and was also an athlete : he took part, for example, in the Ledbury Run † of 1882 and came in fifth, immediately followed by another master, H. N. Fowler ; but, despite his many gifts, his was an unhappy reign, characterized by a sharp decline in numbers.

The cause can undoubtedly be found in the relationship between Cruttwell and Drew. Drew had been housemaster of No. 2 for sixteen years, ever since the College was opened ; and he was the only member of Faber's original staff still at the school. His deep personal affection for his old headmaster emerged clearly from the speech he made on the occasion of Faber's retirement. He found Cruttwell less to his liking ; and in June 1881 the Headmaster felt compelled to bring before the Council several acts of 'insubordination' on the part of Drew, occasions when the latter had refused to implement certain administrative decisions that had been made by Cruttwell. The Council unanimously supported the Headmaster

---

★ It was probably as the result of this connection with Bradfield that this should have been the first school which Malvern played at football. These matches were played in 1882 and 1883, but were then abandoned in favour of the Radley match which became a regular fixture until the First World War. The Bradfield matches were resumed in 1915. The matches with Repton go back to 1894 and those with Shrewsbury to 1896.

† This gruelling eight-mile run from Ledbury over the Hills to Malvern was run for the first time in 1879.

and warned Drew that he was bound to obey. This did not help. In July the Council had to threaten Drew with dismissal, whereupon Drew enlisted the aid of parents of the boys in his house. He had established a strong connection in Exeter, whose Mayor had two sons in No. 2. On behalf of a group of Exeter parents, the Mayor wrote to the Council in support of Drew ; and when, at the end of that summer term, Cruttwell at last dismissed Drew, the Mayor headed a deputation to the Council, which of course could not give in to their pressure. But the consequence was that twenty-eight boys in No. 2 were prematurely withdrawn, about a dozen going with Drew to Leamington College.* Drew had been enormously popular — (in the nets he used to put sixpences on the middle stump behind him, which went to the bowler who could dislodge them. 'He regularly lost about half a crown in the process', writes the son of a boy in his house) — and Old Malvernians no less than parents began to agitate on his behalf ; so that, despite a letter to all parents informing them that not only the Council but all the other assistant masters approved of what Cruttwell had done, the repercussions were not confined to No. 2. What made matters more difficult was that the Rev. T. H. Belcher, the housemaster of No. 1, left at the same time to become headmaster of Brighton College, and the numbers in his house likewise decreased. With No. 2 down from fifty-six boys to twenty-two, it was not easy to find a successor to Drew. The boys in the house were distributed among other houses for a term until C. Graham, a Fellow of Caius and Third Wrangler, could be induced by the remission of two-thirds of the rent for a year to take over the house — incidentally as the first layman to be a housemaster. He stayed for only two years before returning to Cambridge, so that conditions in No. 2 remained unsettled ; and it was ten or eleven years before the house was full again.

---

* An advertisement in the register of a local estate agent in September 1881 shows that Drew planned to open a rival establishment, to be called the New College, Malvern, at the end of the month ; but nothing came of this.

It is not surprising that in 1881 the Council had to report the biggest deficit since the crisis in 1871.* In May 1882 the College was again compelled to ask debenture holders to forgo interest for two years. Cruttwell gave up the capitation fee at a time when he still had a capitation fee to give up, and he also contributed £100 towards the salary of one of the masters. The number and value of scholarships was reduced. None of this helped. Numbers steadily drifted lower until in 1885 they fell below two hundred. Housemasters felt the pinch. They petitioned for a remission of their rent ; and the Rev. G. E. Mackie, who had succeeded Belcher in No. 1, suffered such heavy financial losses that he resigned his house after six years in 1887.

Perhaps it was a sense of inadequacy as a headmaster or perhaps it was his marriage in August 1884 which led Cruttwell to resign and accept a living in Sutton, Surrey. The Council paid tribute to him on his resignation ; and indeed Cruttwell had many virtues. He had a generous nature : that could be seen not only in the financial sacrifices he made voluntarily, but also in his suggestion, when Drew died at Leamington in 1883 ('of a heart broken by his severance from the School he loved so well', one of his family wrote later), that a memorial tablet should be put up to him in Chapel.

Cruttwell was a very able teacher, and indeed the academic performance of the school is a gleam of light in this otherwise sombre period. He taught the Classical Sixth and in his last year as headmaster had the satisfaction of seeing six of his pupils win classical scholarships at the universities. 'Too much the scholar and too little the man of the world', was Toppin's somewhat breezy comment on him.[1] Certainly a headmaster of exceptional all-round ability was now needed if the fortunes of the College were to be restored.

* The expenditure included £400 for the purchase of the chemistry apparatus which Drew had built up at his own expense.

THE REV. W. GRUNDY, HEADMASTER
1885 to 1891

THE REV. C. T. CRUTTWELL, HEADMASTER
1880 to 1885

CHAPTER IV

The Headmastership of W. Grundy
1885–1891

LIKE Faber and Cruttwell, the new headmaster was still in his thirties when he was appointed. The Rev. William Grundy, a Fellow of Worcester College, Oxford, had been a master at Rossall and in 1880 had become headmaster of Warwick School. That school had only eight pupils at the time he took it over, but inside three years he had raised its numbers to seventy boarders and fifty-four day boys. He then applied to his Governors for permission to build a new boarding-house, but they refused. 'Mr Grundy had no intention of wasting his genius for organization and development over a small school if not supported by the governing body in developing it,' writes the historian of Warwick School,[1] and we can well believe that his record there was decisive in securing his appointment to the headmastership of Malvern.

Like Faber also, Grundy was an all-rounder. He was a fine scholar — during his time at Malvern he published a book on Aristotelianism (1889) — and a superb athlete : 'as a fives player he had few equals in England', writes the Rev. A. H. James in the *Malvern Register*.[2] He made frequent and effective use of the cane and was an awe-inspiring disciplinarian. One O.M. remembers vividly the drama of an expulsion, after two boys had been seen by a master late at night in the town. 'Next morning the whole School was called to Big School, empty except for the platform at the end, and we stood in two unarranged masses along the walls. Grundy and the staff, in cap and gown, came on to the platform, and the two boys were brought in in the charge of the Corps Sergeant and stood before them. Grundy then addressed us. I forget what he said, but I knew that the crime reeked to heaven. (They had been playing billiards, in fact.) And lastly — and I can hear it now, for Grundy had that curious utterance, something like "Phmm", which some Scotch and North-countrymen have — he said, "Phmm ! We — do — not — want — you — amongst — us. You — can — go." (All that should be in capital letters.) And down the centre alley-way they went — sort of running the gauntlet without violence. It was all very frightening to a thirteen-year-old, and I suppose was meant to be.'

But the characteristic which above all others made Grundy exactly the headmaster the school needed at this point was that he enjoyed working out a problem — whether at chess (he had played for the University) or in administration. The problems that faced him at Malvern were severe enough to test this quality to the utmost.

Numbers had not yet reached their lowest ebb : this was not until his sixth term in 1887, when they were 188. That year, therefore, there was another appeal to the debenture holders not to exact interest for another ten years : 'Any action taken on the part of the debenture holders would only be an obstacle to the success of the College to which alone they can look for any ultimate value in their security.'

And then, dramatically, the situation improved. Later that year the number reached 211 ; in 1888 they were 220 ; in 1889 they were 244 ; in 1890 274 ; in 1891 323. Exactly what measures Grundy took to achieve this transformation is today far from clear. Some we do know about. In 1888 he intro-duced an Army Class. It was soon afterwards entrusted to E. C. Bullock (O.M.), who was an inspired and very popular teacher and was to teach the Army side brilliantly for forty-three years. Already by 1892 Malvern was one of the half-dozen schools at the top of the list for successes in the Army Examination.[3] Then, in 1890, a class was started in which Book-keeping and Commerce were taught. This probably attracted

THE CRICKET XI AGAINST THE MASTERS, 1891

Back row, from left to right: H. K. Foster, H. H. House, L. S. Milward, E. C. Bullock, Dr. Brockatt (the school doctor), Paul Foley (not on the staff), C. T. Salisbury.

Middle row, from left to right: G. A. Mitchell, P. H. Latham, R. E. Lyon, Rev. W. Grundy, C. Toppin, H. M. Faber, Rev. H. E. Huntington, C. H. Ransome.

Front row, from left to right: J. C. Swinburne, T. B. Rhodes, F. W. Ronney, W. W. Lowe, H. S. Pike, C. J. Jones, W. L. Foster.

some parents who might not have sent their sons to public schools at all.

The growth of the school and the departure of some of the older members of the staff into retirement or headmasterships enabled Grundy to bring in some young blood. Among the new masters H. W. Smith,* Charles Toppin, R. E. Lyon (O.M.), E. C. Bullock (O.M.), H. H. House, and L. S. Milward (O.M.) were to serve Malvern for many years and to become characters whom generations of Malvernians now alive remember with affection. Incidentally, the staff was becoming increasingly lay. Whereas there had been only nine laymen among Faber's twenty-five appointments, there were only two clergy among Grundy's sixteen.

. In 1891 there was a flurry of building activity to meet the needs of these increased numbers. The old Building Company, which had financed this kind of work in the early years, existed no more ; and the remarkable feature of this phase of expansion was the confidence with which Grundy and Foster invested their own money to increase the accommodation. Foster enlarged No. 5 at his own cost to enable him to take ten more boys, and Grundy did the same for School House to take another fifteen. In each case the Council promised to buy the new buildings whenever Grundy or Foster would vacate them. Even No. 2, which did not at first share in the boom and whose housemaster had £50 of his rent remitted as late as 1890 on account of 'the paucity of numbers in the House', now filled up to capacity ; and it became clear that a sixth house would now be needed. For the time being a house called 'Malvernbury' — once a hydropathic establishment ⁴— in Abbey Road was rented from Mr C. W. Dyson Perrins : † H. W. Smith became its first housemaster. Grundy did not intend to rely on rented accommodation any longer than necessary. He bought the land between the existing grounds

* He came with Grundy from Warwick, where he had been the headmaster's assistant.

† He was the son of one of the original partners in Lea & Perrins and in later years became one of the most generous benefactors of the school.

and the railway line and proposed to build No. 6 on part of it, the Council agreeing to become his tenant for £300 a year.

It was also no longer possible to allow the Sanatorium to take up class-room space in the Main Building. Here, too, accommodation was initially rented, at 2, The Lees, pending the building of a new one. The Chapel had also to be enlarged : in short, growing numbers brought their own problems, and Grundy could jocularly say on Speech Day of 1890 that the school was 'threatened' with further increases in the coming terms. But he was clearly exhilarated by this sudden turn in the school's fortunes. He and Foster set on foot a subscription list to pay for a Swimming Bath, and this building, in its mock-Tudor shell, soon took shape at the bottom of the school grounds.

The school was now becoming sufficiently well known to receive distinguished visitors. Lord Randolph Churchill, who had shared Grundy's passion for chess at Oxford, came to the Speech Day of 1889 ; and the first royal visitors came in 1891, in the persons of the Duke and Duchess of Teck and Princess May (the later Queen Mary). And it was felt that the school was now sufficiently advanced in years and importance to have a song of its own instead of the Winchester 'Domum'. On Speech Day of 1888 the 'Carmen' was first sung. Its Latin words were written by M. A. Bayfield and set to music by R. E. Lyon ; whilst a third member of the staff, C. W. Horsburgh, provided the ingenious English translation which, hardly known today, is appended to assist those modern Malvernians who find difficulty in translating the original.*
Malvernians of 1888 will, on the whole, have found the task a little easier, since more of them read Classics ; but even then there was alarm at the inroads that modern studies were making on a classical education ; and Lord Randolph Churchill in his speech, probably not aware of his host's innovations, deplored this tendency with arguments which, indeed, the school had heard from other visiting speakers on occasion.

* Appendix C.

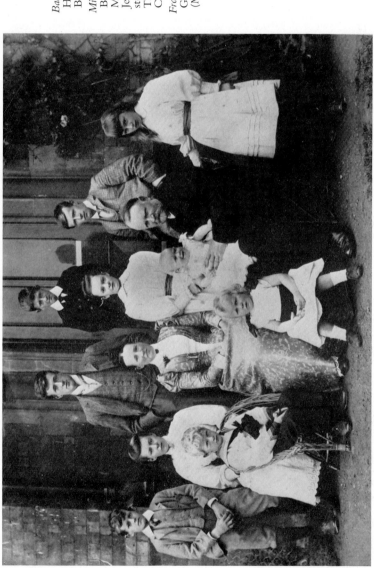

Back row, from left to right: Harry (H. K.), Tip (R. E.), Billy (W. L.)

Middle row, from left to right: Basil (B. S.), Mabel (later Mrs. Bullock), Mrs. Foster, Jessie (later Mrs. Greenstock), Johnny (N. J. A.), The Rev. Henry Foster, Cecily

Front row, from left to right: Geoffrey (G. N.), Maurice (M. K.)

THE REV. HENRY FOSTER AND HIS FAMILY, 1891

Academically the standard of the school was not, until Grundy's last year, very high. Already in Cruttwell's time the *Malvernian* had lost the high quality of its early numbers. In Grundy's it contained little else than lengthy reports on games. If the tone of what the boys wrote in editorials and correspondence at all reflects the opinion of the school in general, they found little to interest them apart from games.

Of course, under Toppin's guidance the standard of cricket was beginning to rise. In 1891 the Repton match was won for the first time in thirteen years. In P. H. Latham, a future Cambridge cricket captain, Malvern produced the first of its long line of cricket blues, and the Foster brothers were beginning their remarkable athletic career. In 1890, while still at school, the seventeen-year-old H. K. Foster played for Worcestershire against the Free Foresters and made 179, the largest score for the county in the last ten years; and the partnership between him and his brother W. L. Foster, which was to win them the Public Schools Rackets Cup in 1892, was just beginning.

All this is chronicled fully. On the other hand, university scholarships are sparse on the ground in most of those years and the Debating Society suspended its activities. But then there was suddenly a sharp improvement here, too : one of Grundy's new masters, the Rev. H. E. Huntington (O.M.),* started a Literary Society in 1890 and in 1891 revived the Debating Society (which was soon to approve of the Conservative Government of the time and to condemn Trade Unions). But, above all, there was a sudden increase in university awards. In Grundy's last year, eight boys won scholarships and exhibitions at Oxford and Cambridge. In that year, Malvern was excelled in this respect by only eight other schools in England.[5]

The news of the last of these awards reached Grundy on his death-bed. On December 1, 1891, he was playing a game of rackets when he was seized with paralysis. Four

* He died of pneumonia in 1893 after only four years on the staff, at the age of thirty-two.

days later he died. All the boys had to file past his corpse.

The account of his Headmastership makes it clear that it was a decisive one in the history of the school. For the first time it looked as if Malvern might in time become prosperous ; though it must be remembered that other Victorian foundations were by this time full, and there was room at Malvern for at least another two hundred and fifty boys. All the same, in a short four years an astonishing transformation had been wrought ; and when the tide began to turn, Grundy, confident that this was no temporary improvement, acted with confidence and vigour. 'Cynics may have called him an opportunist,' wrote Toppin, 'but then the successful Headmaster must possess some such quality. Let us rather say that he amply illustrated the School motto.'*

It was not only the school which benefited from his vigour. As if headmastering was not enough to satisfy his energy, he had been Chairman of the Local Government Board during the last four years of his life. In that post he was succeeded by Dr. Pike, the School Doctor. Dr. Pike was therefore a most fitting person to raise a memorial subscription from Grundy's friends in the town and the school for the creation of the school library which bears his name.†

* The school motto, 'Sapiens Qui Prospicit', is said to have been invented by Dr. Sewell, the Warden of New College — it is not a quotation from the Classics — and to have been suggested to Faber, who adopted it before the College opened. The crest, designed by Sir Edmund Lechmere, was adopted in 1877. 'The three fountains represent the three chief wells of Malvern, probably, to judge from the old guide books, the Chalybeate Spring (now lost to sight in the garden of Oakdale), St. Anne's Well, and the Holy Well, and may be held to symbolize the three founts of learning, Classics, Mathematics, and Natural Science. The five torteaux were no doubt taken from the arms of the See of Worcester in which there are ten. They are sometimes said to represent the wafers at the Host, though their actual origin appears to be uncertain.' (From the Malvernian Society's List of Members, 1961.) The animal holding a weather vane in the crest is a Gryphon and is taken from the stone figures that originally decorated the gable ends of the College buildings and of School House.

† It was housed in what had been the Sanatorium and is now the Art School. It was one place in the school where a boy could not be fagged, and so, until the creation of the Memorial Library in 1925, the only sanctuary for the studious-minded. (C. S. Lewis, *Surprised by Joy*, p. 112.) H. W. Smith had the exciting and responsible task of building up the new library.

those days purely voluntary, and it had been rather languishing in the days when the school was small. But as numbers rose, so did the membership of the Corps. In June 1897, on the occasion of Queen Victoria's Diamond Jubilee, a contingent went to Windsor where the Queen reviewed the Public School Volunteers. It was a hot afternoon and many of the contingent, in their dark-blue uniforms and heavy busbies, were acutely aware of the burning sun ; but in those days, before television had brought the Sovereign into every home, a sight of the Queen at the height of the mystique which surrounded her was a unique experience for a boy and might well sweep away any grudging feelings he might have had that the Queen had found it impossible earlier that year to grant the request from the Head of School for an additional week's holiday. Her secretary had replied that 'it is deemed advisable to leave the decision of a question of this nature to the responsible authorities of your College'. These had given the extra week in due course.

Numbers at the school continued to rise. In 1893 they topped 400; and when Gray retired there were about 100 more boys on the books than there had been when he came. And yet behind all this there were new and serious financial crises.

These came suddenly and unexpectedly. Indeed, in 1893 the College had resumed payment of interest on its debentures at three per cent, to rise to four per cent as soon as the accumulated losses had been reduced to £5,000. This, it was anticipated, would not take long ; but these hopes were soon dashed.

As one reads through the day-to-day work of the College in the Council minutes, one is constantly struck by the amount of time that was taken up by discussion of malodorous drains and allied sanitary matters. Very properly, every such complaint was remedied ; but it was never long before it cropped up again. Then, in October 1893, inspectors reported grave defects in the laying of the drains of Nos. 1 and 2. Work on them was immediately started. Then, in December, a boy from No. 5 developed diphtheria as soon as he arrived home. As all the other houses were inspected during the Christmas holidays, defects in the drains were found all over the College ; but there was no time to undertake any major work before the boys returned. In March a drain was opened in connection with building the new cricket pavilion, just by the Grub Shop. Diphtheria struck again. Four boys and George Arber caught it. Two boys died of it. The school was sent home early for the third time in its history,* and the opening of the new term was postponed for nearly a fortnight while all the drains were taken up and relaid. The original estimate for this work was £1,700 ; but in the end the cost mounted to £7,500, a sum which could be raised only by borrowing. It would of course be quite wrong to think of this crisis in financial terms only. In the days before diphtheria inoculation, an outbreak of this disease in any community was a most frightening and harrowing experience — 'like some dark cloud, spreading its fear over them', said Gray; and on the following Speech Day he said that it would take a lifetime wholly to do away with the memory of the sorrow and the anxiety arising from the state of suspense in which they had all been. It was, he said, a sorrow through which one might pass once, but hardly twice.†

The second blow to the finances of the College was delivered by the Urban District Council. There was a bridle road across the College property, between the swimming

---

* The first time was after an outbreak of scarlet fever in 1869 ; the second after the death of Grundy. In the two years following the diphtheria outbreak, 1895 and 1896, the school had to be sent home before the end of the spring term because of virulent influenza epidemics.

† Wellington College had had an outbreak of diphtheria two years earlier, in 1892. There the repairs which had to be made to the drainage system were so extensive that the school had to be evacuated ; and it spent the Easter term at the Imperial Hotel in Malvern. (David Newsome, *A History of Wellington College*, pp. 215-220.) At Malvern College there was to be another outbreak of diphtheria in 1904, in James' time. There were four cases in No. 2, and that House was sent home for three weeks while the building was disinfected. The source of the infection was a maid who had brought it in from outside the school.

baths and the cricket field ; and the Urban District Council now intimated that it was proposed to turn this into a properly metalled road and that the College was legally responsible for the cost thereof. The cost was, of course, not the only consideration : the College did not want to have a public road running right across the grounds. But the only way of avoiding this was to pay for a new road to link Albert Road with Court Road, and this would involve making a bridge through the railway embankment. It was the course that the College eventually decided to take. It paid approximately £2,300 for the construction of most of what is today Woodshears Road and for the railway bridge which passes over it.

These unexpected expenses were all the more disturbing since the expansion of the College demanded more building. The Council had already undertaken to buy land and to build a Sanatorium on it. The money for this was borrowed. The cost of the beds and the general running of the Sanatorium was still borne by the housemasters. With the death of Grundy there had died his plan to build No. 6 at his own cost. Since the extra accommodation was urgently wanted, the Council now undertook to build the house. The money for this, too, had to be borrowed ; but in 1894 Toppin, who had taken over 'Malvernbury' from Smith,* was able to move his boys into the new premises — the house which is today known as No. 5. Nos. 7 and 8 had their origins at about the same time. They were houses which were already rented by their housemasters. The house in The Lees where R. E. Lyon lived became No. 7 in 1892 ; and in 1895 C. T. Salisbury turned 'Malvernhurst', his house in Priory Road, into No. 8. The addition of these houses, therefore, cost the College very little.

Other additions to the school in those years were a large cricket pavilion to replace the old lean-to shed, and a new Grub Shop. (O.M.s will find nothing wrong with this

---

* Smith had given up the house because of ill-health, but fortunately remained on the teaching staff for many years to come.

inelegant nomenclature ; but G. E. Martin, the Chairman of the Council,* found the word sufficiently distasteful to alter it to 'Refreshment Shop' in the minutes.) Both these new additions were paid for out of the profits of the Grub Shop, which since 1878 had, at Foster's instigation, been run as an independent venture whose profits were to be devoted to develop the amenities of the school. Gray, at his own cost, built a Chemical Laboratory in the same block (today the Maths block) ; † but towards the end of his Headmastership his principal object was the building of a new chapel. The old chapel in the south wing of the Main Building was becoming too small ; and besides, the space was needed for classrooms. But there was no hope that the College finances, burdened as they were by recent borrowing, could make any contributions.‡ Gray therefore opened a Chapel Fund with a donation of £500. By the middle of 1896 over £6,000 had been subscribed ; and in June of that year a bazaar was held to bring in more money. For three days the College was given over to entertaining visitors. The programme laid on by the school included a performance on the Terrace of *A Midsummer-Night's Dream* ; the story of the Oresteia displayed in living tableaux by the Classical Department ; and a display of 'Living Waxworks' by the less classically minded. There was an 'Assault at Arms' (a gymnastic performance), and a 'Café Chantant' in which masters, boys, and friends of the school provided music, 'though the necessary flow of conversation tended at times to spoil the enjoyment of the

---

* Earl Beauchamp had died in February 1891. His heir, the seventh Earl, was still a minor ; and Martin, senior partner of an important banking firm, who had been Treasurer of the Council since its earliest days, was elected Chairman. The seventh Earl was elected a member of the Council in 1895 and became Chairman on the death of Martin ten years later.

† Today's Armoury had been the Gymnasium since 1876, and there had been a workshop in the same block since 1877. The money for both was raised by voluntary contributions.

‡ It even declined to spend £8 a year on installing and running a telephone in the College in 1896, though the Sanatorium got one in 1897. In 1901 the Council considered a second-hand typewriter for the College — at 10 guineas — an unnecessary luxury.

music-lovers'.[1] The Art Master, Mr Ehrke, who had had
pictures hung at the Royal Academy, arranged an art exhibition in which his own paintings were duly hung. Earl
Beauchamp lent a collection of snuff boxes, and Mr Dyson
Perrins a collection of curious watches. There were lectures
on The New Photography (meaning X-rays) by the Science
Master, Mr Berridge, at the end of whose lectures 'many
visitors took a gruesome pleasure in laying bare their bones
to the gaze of others'. A phonograph enabled visitors to gain
amusement 'in listening to Gladstone's speech, in Edison's
wonderful invention, and also in hearing the principal comic
songs of the day'. Films were shown on a contraption known
as the Kinetoscope, where the figures were so lifelike 'that
visitors might imagine they were really in the Gaiety Theatre'.
These are only some of the activities into which the school
threw itself with immense zest and with all the unsophisticated
excitement of boys who did not yet take the marvels of science
for granted. The bazaar made a profit of £1,500. Half the
estimated cost of the chapel had now been raised ; and before
he retired Gray had the satisfaction of seeing the plans of Sir
Arthur Blomfield for a handsome chapel to seat 650 people
and of seeing work begun on the site of what had been until
then masters' tennis courts.

There is no doubt that the building of the Chapel meant
more to Gray than a practical necessity. He was keenly aware
of the work the Church had to do ; and in no field was this
more evident than in the expansion that took place during his
time in the Mission Work of the College. So far, the school
had given financial help to the Vicar of the Parish of All
Saints, Haggerston, in the East End of London. But by now
the College was ready to do more than this : it wanted to
appoint a missioner of its own, as several other public schools
were doing at about this time ; and since the scope in Haggerston was comparatively small, it started instead a Mission in
Canning Town, a parish of 7,000 people. The Rev. Gresham
Gillett was appointed Missioner, and the College contributed

£200 a year towards his work. Each term Gillett came over to Malvern to talk to the boys about the work of the Mission : the opening of Boys' Clubs, of a Working Men's Club, and of a Church Lads' Brigade ; the holding of Sunday Schools attended by 250 or 300 children ; the building of a corrugated iron church ; the work of the Mission Nurse who visited and tended the sick. He would describe the conditions of life in that part of the East End : heavy unemployment, especially among the boys too old to remain at school and too young to tackle the heavy work of a docker ; then the casual labour in the docks when they became older ; the struggle with the management of the Board Schools, usually in nonconformist hands, when he wanted to withdraw the children for the hour of religious instruction for which the Education Acts provided. Many of the Malvern boys who listened to Gillett probably remained rather indifferent, reflecting in this the average run of humanity. Kennedy-Cox records in his *Autobiography* [2] that he was frankly bored — but some were stirred, and in 1893 the prefects gave £20 to the Mission.

As the school grew in numbers and in age, so did its Old Boys. In the early years, meetings of the Old Boys were few, generally small, and irregular. But by the 1890s there were already over 2,000 Old Malvernians, and the oldest of these were approaching middle age. Gray was always particularly glad to welcome them back to the school and was a frequent visitor to O.M. reunions in other places. In 1894 the rather haphazard organization of Old Malvernians gave way to the Old Malvernian Society. Like the O.M. Clubs before, the Society arranged dinners, matches, etc., for its members ; but this was only the last of the objects listed in its rules. Among the other objects were to afford to any benefactor an opportunity of giving or leaving money or property of any kind to the school, for purposes of endowment by way of scholarships or otherwise ; to give assistance to the School Mission ; and to give special prizes. The benefactions of the Society to the school began with the provision of a scholarship of £15 in 1896 and a Science Prize of £5 in 1897.   Few people could have guessed what great things were to flow from these beginnings, though an investment of £1,000 by a wealthy shipowner, Heath Harrison (O.M.), to provide a scholarship at Brasenose was a sign of the generosity with which many Old Malvernians were to come to the help of the school in future years.

In November 1896 Gray became seriously ill.   Some time before, he had inspected the scaffolding of the Chapel and while moving along some high planks had fainted and fallen — fortunately onto some planks just below.   His fainting fit was generally ascribed to the hot weather on that summer's day; but it was probably an attack of the illness which now incapacitated him : auditory vertigo.   For the greater part of two terms Foster was acting headmaster, as he had been in the short interregnum between Grundy and Gray.   In the spring of 1897 Gray returned to work; but within a matter of weeks his illness recurred and he had to resign (though he lived to be eighty-four).

It was sad for the school that it should have lost two able headmasters after each had held office for only five or six years.   Reigning at the close of the Victorian age, Gray represented much of its spirit : the courage, enterprise, and high moral purpose.   And not Gray alone.   The history of a school is so often written in terms of its headmasters that it is easy to forget that they cannot mould the spirit of a school unaided.   In one of his early speeches Gray remarked on the wonderful and remarkable relationship he had found at Malvern between masters and boys ; and, as one reads the records of the time, one cannot help feeling that this was true. There seems to have been very little of the image one has of stern and remote Victorian schoolmasters.   The gaiety of the bazaar scheme could never have been produced by a school whose masters were severe pedagogues.   In the phenomenal winter of 1895 the younger masters could be seen tobogganing together with the boys on the glorious long run from the College building down to the railway line : for once the slope of the ground called for no criticism. Foster, Toppin, Lyon, Smith, Wachter, Bullock, Huntington, House, Milward, Farrant, Berridge, Lowe — there is a warmth in references to these men, not only in the columns of the *Malvernian*, but in the memories of O.M.s. One of them writes of the shock when, in his last year at school, he was caned *for the first time*, and he claims to have been an average boy, not abnormally good nor particularly bad ; and this incident reinforces a feeling that the discipline of the school was not based on fear. True, when beatings did take place, they could be surrounded with dreadful ceremonial. An O.M. of Gray's time writes, 'I suppose I am one of the few remaining people today who saw the last of the "Public Lickings". These were held in the Big School Room, with the whole School present ; and we stood upon painted straight lines which kept order. The College Porter stood by the Headmaster, with the canes.'

But on the whole, discipline was kindly. When a Latin master wrote on the blackboard for translation, 'Shall I stay here or go to Philippi ?', a small boy could sing out, 'For God's sake, Sir, go to Philippi !' without fear of terrible chastisement. When an influenza epidemic struck down a whole form except one boy, the form master and his sole pupil agreed that this was no time for work and played chess instead.

As for the way boys treated each other, O.M.s from two different houses have written that there was never any bullying during this period. A very common feature of only a few years before had been set fights with bare fists during break. The news that such a fight was impending would bring most of the school to the scene in high excitement. But this had been stopped now by the authorities. There were still vigorous scrimmages round the Fives Court just before eight o'clock every morning ; for the only way of booking a Fives Court was to have the name pinned to the door at eight. So a

THE REV. S. R. JAMES, HEADMASTER
1897 to 1914

THE REV. A. ST. J. GRAY, HEADMASTER
1892 to 1897

prefect would organize bands of fags to pin his name on the door and defend it against all bands sent by other prefects until the clock struck eight. This procedure was called 'busking' — 'and what fun it was !' recalls a venerable survivor of those days.

More peaceful was another tradition which grew up at that time and which expressed the harmony and friendliness of the place. On Sunday evenings in the summer, after Chapel, while the masters strolled up and down the centre of the Senior Turf, the boys walked round and round the periphery, always one way, talking and perhaps watching the shadow of the hills lengthening over the Severn Valley as the sun went down. It was in those days, as it has been again since 1958, quite voluntary. In James' day it became compulsory. It was then said that the custom had been started to firm the turf after the original levelling of the Senior ; but in the reminiscences of O.M.s of the 1890s it figures as something very different : a pleasant, relaxed, and sociable occasion and one more small indication that Malvern under Gray was not only a successful school ; it was a happy one as well.

CHAPTER VI

The Headmastership of S. R. James
1897–1914

WHEN the Malvern Cadet Corps paraded at Windsor on Queen Victoria's Jubilee in June 1897, it was drawn up to the right of the Eton contingent, commanded by Major S. R. James. When he came home that evening, he found the telegram informing him that he had been appointed headmaster of Malvern.

James, a scholar of Trinity College, Cambridge, and a former Captain of the Cambridge Rugby XV, had been an assistant master at Eton for eighteen years and a housemaster for eight. There he had taught the sons of G. E. Martin, Chairman of the Malvern College Council,* and also the seventh Earl Beauchamp who was a member of the Council and was to succeed Martin as Chairman on the latter's death in 1905. James' private letters to Beauchamp began, 'My dear Elmley' ; Beauchamp's to James began, 'M' Tutor'.

James himself tells the following story about his appointment : 'There was a large field of candidates ; the final choice lay between my old friend A. H. Cooke, Senior Classic in my year, and myself. I don't know whether the following tale is true or not : but I was afterwards informed that a letter from a mutual friend of Cooke's and mine had some influence in the election. The writer said, "Cooke was never really a boy ; James has never ceased to be one ! ".' [1] *Si non è vero, è ben trovato* : there certainly was something boyish

---

* One of them, G. E. Bromley-Martin, came to teach temporarily at Malvern in 1898.

about James, not only then, when he was forty-two, but later, as reports from O.M.s towards the end of his Headmastership and indeed his own autobiography written at the age of seventy bear witness.

He was thoroughly extrovert and uninhibited, quick-tempered but good-hearted, with a vocabulary that amused those boys that were used to it and scarified those who were not. 'You scrubby dog ; you mouldy toad ; you scruffy fellow,' — these were some of his favourite phrases. The story that he barked at some offending boy, ' What is your scrubby name ?' and received the timid answer, 'James, Sir', is well known to Malvernians of his time ; and though it could be true of seven different boys at Malvern and is indeed reported of several of these, James' autobiography narrates the incident as belonging to his Eton period.[2] 'He had a strong sense of humour,' writes an O.M., 'and one suspects that he thoroughly enjoyed these exhibitions of bad temper, regarding them as a form of histrionic exercise, and that he was not always as angry as his appearance and manner would indicate ; for his black moustache, beetling brows and rather vermilion complexion made his aspect formidable. He was free with the cane, and his technique of flagellation (back-handed, I believe) was said to be more than competent.'

He loved the outdoor life, took some country west of the hills from Lord Beauchamp for shooting on an autumn after-noon, and played golf on an average four times a week, some-times more often.[3] Even on Speech Day he would escape from parents by betaking himself to the golf-links as soon as the ceremony was over. 'He was no cricketer,' writes one who ought to know ; 'but sometimes he could be induced to play.' One such occasion was on his fiftieth birthday when he played against an actors' eleven captained by Sir Frank Benson. The two sides were in collusion to see to it that James should make exactly fifty runs. By dint of some judicious umpiring this aim was achieved, with James apparently only partly aware of what was going on and being heard to say modestly afterwards that cricket was not a very difficult game.★

'Generally speaking,' writes an O.M., 'he was not an imaginative man.' He is said to have reduced poetry to prose and Homer to a page of Bradshaw. Certainly his early speeches on Speech Day were painfully platitudinous and varied hardly at all from year to year. Only towards the end of his career do they become more alive and amusing.

But all of them reveal certain traits in his personality. Though with unfailing regularity he protested that one should not make a religion of games, nevertheless it was this side of school life which manifestly gave him most pleasure ; and indeed no headmaster of Malvern could have failed to delight in these golden days of the school's games history. The seam of Foster brothers was not yet exhausted. B. S., G. N., M. K., and N. J. A. Foster successively followed their three elder brothers through the Cricket XI in the years between 1898 and 1909.† There were other cricketing families. There were S. H. Day who, while still at school, made a century in his first county match, and his brother A. P. Day. Their sister Daisy married Charles Toppin. Then there were the three Naumann brothers. Less dynastically, there was F. T. Mann who in 1922/3 was to captain England against South Africa ; D. J. Knight who got into the School XI as a new boy and in 1921 played for England against Australia ; W. H. B. Evans,

---

★ Benson was in Malvern to play Richard III. When the boys arrived at the Assembly Rooms to see the play and found the front rows occupied by girls from the numerous girls' schools in Malvern, all wearing their hair long or in pig-tails with ribbons, the young gentlemen occupying the row immediately behind managed to tie the hair of the girls to their chairs with the ribbons. 'There was a pretty good noise going on. The mistresses appeared non-plussed.' It was quite a job for the master on duty to get matters disentangled.

† Malvern cricket is the inspiration of P. G. Wodehouse's schoolboy story *Mike at Wrykyn*. The Jackson brothers in that book are taken from the Fosters ; and the climax is, appropriately, the 'Ripton Match'. Wodehouse was not an O.M. ; but, he writes, 'When I was a small boy, I used to spend part of the summer holidays with an uncle who was Vicar of Upton-on-Severn, and I played a lot of boys' cricket, some of it on the Malvern ground. From those early years the place fascinated me. I was of course cricket-mad in those days, and I can well remember peering in at the pavilion and reading all those illustrious names on the boards.'

later captain of Oxford, whom E. W. Swanton described as possibly the greatest Malvern all-rounder [4] and a memorial tablet to whom was put into the chapel after he was killed flying with Cody in 1913 ; W. S. Bird, who was to keep wicket for Oxford and the Gentlemen ; and several other future Blues and County Players — all these played wonderfully for the school and made Malvern cricket famous throughout the country. Those were the days when cricket enthusiasts talked about 'Fostershire' when the brothers played for the county and when R. E. Foster set up a new Test Match record of 287 in Australia in 1903 and captained England against South Africa in 1907. The Fosters also kept up the family tradition in Rackets : B. S. Foster and W. H. B. Evans won the Public Schools Rackets Competition in 1900, and in 1908 M. K. and N. J. A. Foster did likewise. In Football also the O.M.s kept the name of the school before the public. R. E. Foster captained England against Wales in 1902 and so achieved the unique distinction of having captained England in both cricket and football. In 1905 both Varsity sides were captained by O.M.s and five others played in that match. In 1909 and 1912 the O.M.s won the Arthur Dunn Cup and in 1911 the A.F.A. Cup. No wonder that, with the reputation of Malvern Association football so dazzling, Rugby football, introduced in 1910, should be confined in effect to the Easter term, with snow, influenza, and athletics all cutting down the time that could be devoted to it. With James, Henry Foster, Toppin, and Lowe all being enthusiastic players of Golf, that game, too, flourished : in 1904 five out of the sixteen players in the Varsity Golf Match were O.M.s. Finally, this recital of athletic achievement should include A. N. S. Jackson, the Olympic Gold Medallist in the 1,500 metres at Stockholm in 1912.

What headmaster whose school achieved such a record could bring himself to play this down on public occasions, even if he had wanted to ? But it is not surprising that the school should begin to get a reputation as primarily a games school ; that parents with athletically promising boys should be keen to send them to Malvern ; that boys, always ready to worship games-players, should do so more than ever when their gods played before more than local spectators. There is overwhelming evidence that games were taken desperately seriously, and that not only by the boys. The following anecdote may serve as an example : it is told by an O.M. master who was himself a distinguished cricketer, not by one whose days were made wretched by his inability to play games :

'In those days it was customary for the whole house to have sausages for tea on the evening of a victorious house-match. I suppose they were kept for Sunday breakfast if the match was lost ! (Breakfast in my day was porridge, bread and butter only. For 30/- a term you could have a cooked breakfast, but very few had it then. I never thought of asking my parents to let me have it ; it was not done.)* I can remember Mr Bryans, housemaster of No. 4, at one of the first housematches I ever watched, striding up and down the touch line shouting, "Sausages for tea, boys ! Sausages for tea !" I believe he really thought it spurred his team to greater endeavour. But if your House won *the Final*, your housemaster had to provide not merely sausages but a slap-up house-supper, turkey or fowl of some sort, ham, tongue and all the rest.

'Now one year the House Final was between School House and the favourite, another house. In fact it was felt that this other house could not help winning. The housemaster of this other house will be Mr. X.

'The Final was played, and contrary to all form, S.H. won. That of course put Sydney James in a spot. No provision for a house supper had been made, so what to do ? Only an hour or two to make good !

'Mr. X, as you will hear, apparently was worried too,

---

* Note that this remark refers to the writer's schooldays round about 1890. An O.M. who was a boy twenty years later writes that 'luckily all the parents paid up'.

though he had made lavish preparations for the victory which had eluded him.

'A small School House boy had just reached the Terrace on the way back from the match when he met Sydney James.

' "Hi! boy!,", says James. "Go to No. So-and-So and ask to be taken to Mr. X and give him this message from me in these words. 'Mr. James wants to know how much you will take for your house-supper.' "

'It hardly sounds as if at the moment they were on very good terms ! Unless, as is just possible, and in fact would have been very sensible, a deal *had* been done.

'Off went the boy, rang the bell, asked directly for Mr. X to give him a message from the Head, and was shown into the study. He gave his message — he did not really know what it all meant at the time — verbatim.

'Mr. X flushed, got up, and said, "did the damned fellow send me a message like that ?" A pause, and then, "Well, come with me and then go back and tell him what you have seen."

'Off they went through the house to a door at the back leading into the garden, where a good deal of movement was going on. Remember the match had been over a bare hour. Across one end of the garden, the gardener had been told to dig a trench, and white-aproned maids and servants were busily depositing in it the viands which should have graced the festive board at the expected house supper !

'Talk about saving face ! The Orientals aren't in it. It does make one think, doesn't it ?'

Indeed it does. And when the housemaster was popular, as this one was, and so cast down by the defeat of his house, what an example he set ! Keyed up for every match, the boys may have taken their defeats with outward stoicism as became a good loser ; but they certainly took them hard. Here is a description from the pen of a famous cricketer, E. R. T. Holmes, writing of a slightly later period :

'Oh, those Junior House Matches ! Could anything be

more frightening, with one's Housemaster, F. U. Mugliston ("Mugs" for short) and all the Prefects watching ? All the rest of the boys in the House were there too, and so were the Matron, the odd-job man (whose name was Tetzel) and the bootboy. And they were all madly partisan. A sort of "Don't, for goodness' sake, let the House down" atmosphere seemed to take us by the throat, and this was almost sickening for us small boys, most of whom were very indifferent cricketers. For me, already something of a prodigy, the position was even worse, because the reputation of the entire House apparently dangled from my youthful shoulders. If I failed, so did the others. Always, in these ghastly matches, I was petrified, and one of these nightmares is worth recording.

'It occurred in 1921, when, having won my "first eleven" colours at the age of fifteen, I was still eligible to play for the Junior House side. On this occasion my House was called upon to make forty-one runs to win the match. On the evening prior to our attempt to make this formidable fourth innings total, a touring company from the Arts League of Service gave a performance in the gymnasium, and the entire school had fallen in love with a little girl who, dressed in crinolines and carrying a parasol, sang a song which may have been "Pretty little Polly Perkins from Paddington Green", but may equally well have been something else. The following morning "Bingo Banks", one of the assistant masters, asked me to tea that afternoon, saying that one of the members of the company of the previous evening was also coming. I accepted, but added that I might be a trifle late, as I was playing in a Junior House Match. "Oh," said he, "you'll soon polish them off; you've only got to make forty-one."

'As it happened, we were all out for thirty-nine ! Clearly it was my fault, and I thanked heaven that I had to go out to tea with "Bingo", thus avoiding the rest of the House — at least temporarily !

'I changed and sauntered out of the School grounds, along Priory Road to Bingo's lodgings, feeling in very low spirits.

He opened the door, "Ah, there you are, Holmes ; come in. Now I expect you remember this little lady singing to us last night. Her name is Hermione Baddeley."

'When I returned to the House, our defeat no longer mattered. I had met HER, and I had regained my lost prestige.' [5]

Here is another account from an O.M. The writer was a scholar who was not happy at the school where, he says, 'the Philistines were in their glory'. But he tried to conform, at least in some respects, as the following will show. He begins by writing about his housemaster, C. T. Salisbury :

'The housemaster of the house to which I was allocated did not cultivate games as assiduously as some of his colleagues. Most honourable and God-fearing of men, he was a Cincinnatus by disposition, a lover of the simple life, and as often as not in his spare time he would be spied half-way up a tree in his large and beautiful garden, practising the art of pruning. He thus failed to draw those boys whose ambitions were athletic, but did attract a high proportion of scholars whose parents presumably had little or no choice in the matter of houses. It so came about that his house was somewhat despised, both on account of its lack of numbers, for his house was never full, and its failure to win athletic distinction. The fact that its members were strongly represented in the Sixth Form did not add to the prestige of the house, which was somehow in the position of a poor relation. We tried hard to improve our status, and in my last year reached the final of the house football competition. The ground was very muddy and slithery, and it is curious how I reproach myself bitterly, more than thirty years later, for stupidly failing to have the worn studs on my football boots renewed before the match — not that the result would have been materially affected. It is indeed remarkable how, in defiance of logic and inner conviction, one was elated or depressed by the results of house, but especially school matches. In my first summer term, after a good start, the Malvern cricket eleven was skittled out by Repton in the second innings for seventy-seven runs, and decisively beaten. That day one's heart sank almost as low as it was to sink in the hour of France's fall, or when the *Prince of Wales* and *Repulse* sailed forth with high resolve, to meet a sudden doom. . . .

'It is not for me to decry the cult of games, remembering as I do the victorious school eleven of 1910, and those two gallant bowlers, Scott and Burton — poor short-lived Scott, victim of that earlier war, Scott of the golden hair and flashing smile, fit model for Praxiteles, charging up to the wicket with godlike strides to deliver his thunderbolt, and the gentle, wily Burton, with his fascinating action and subtle variations of speed and flight ; no, not for me, with memories of the stylish Donald Knight, and the elegance and panache of the elder Naumann, his exuberant drives past cover, and his square cuts that made the boundary rails resound.'

The author of the above extract could at least play football and appreciate the poetry of cricket. Critical though he was, he was capable of being caught up in the joy and despair of Malvern games-players. From C. S. Lewis, though, for whom the whole cult was utterly repulsive, comes this summing up :

'The truth is that organized and compulsory games had, in my day, banished the element of play from school life almost entirely. There was no time to play (in the proper sense of the word). The rivalry was too fierce, the prizes too glittering, the "hell of failure" too severe.' [6]

There may be some Old Malvernians who find all this very exaggerated, and for them it very well may be. But stories that possibly Malvern took its games unduly seriously were current in the outside world long before some well-known authors relieved themselves rather publicly of their suppressed unhappiness some thirty or forty years later. In 1904, for instance, in the *Saturday Review*, an article on Malvern which is on the whole highly laudatory — praising especially the absence of ancient traditions, which in turn promoted 'an absence of convention and a real adaptability which, when combined, as it so often seems to be, with downright, strenuous activity, is the making of any school' — this same article feels bound to say, 'If we have any criticism to make, it is that the athletic is too elaborate and almost overdone, and though the scholarship list is a very fair one, the standard of work throughout the school might possibly be somewhat higher.'*   The article, however, continues, 'If this be so, we feel sure the Head has his eye upon the defect ; but the Headmaster is emphatic that athletic distinction is by no means necessary, as it is at many schools, for positions of influence : of the twenty to twenty-five school prefects probably at any one time a half could not be classified as athletes at all :† for the post of prefect character is the sole qualification, reaching sixth form being no more necessarily a passport than getting into the XI.'

But James was worried by the criticism. 'It makes me angry when I hear it said, as I have more than once heard it said, that Malvern is a school where too much attention is paid to games', he told the parents in 1912, on a Speech Day to which, as will be seen below, he had asked Ranjitsinhji, 'The Prince of Cricket', to give away the prizes. 'I do not believe that it is in the least true.'

Indeed, the performance in university scholarship examinations remained good, mainly as the result of the classical teaching of H. H. House. 'He had curly brown hair, bright blue eyes, which were often cast ceilingwards, and the general appearance of a superannuated cherub', writes a former pupil of his. 'This aesthetic, highly impersonal individual, with his scholarly stoop, high-pitched voice and occasional spoonerism, lived in his own world and was impervious to his surroundings. It was the world of the spirit, the cult of beauty which really mattered. He conducted us through his beloved Georgics with a light of ecstasy in his eyes. The *Golden Treasury* was his constant companion. His exquisitely neat handwriting

---

* January 2, 1904.
† In fact, of the twenty-six school prefects in office when this article appeared, twenty-two were at least members of their house eleven before they left school. Ten reached the Sixth Form.

denoted the life-long Hellenist ; the taste and elegance of his Greek iambics could scarcely have been surpassed.' He ran a flourishing Literary Society which met in his house (No. 4) to read plays ; and today the Sixth Form class-room is panelled in his memory.

But the most beloved of the non-athletic masters was H. W. Smith, 'Smugy' as he was nicknamed — but C. S. Lewis, to ensure that the word should be correctly pronounced ('the first syllable should rhyme exactly with *Fugue'*), spelt it 'Smewgy'. Here is his tribute : 'Smewgy was "beyond expectation, beyond hope". He was a grey-head with large spectacles and a wide mouth which combined to give him a frog-like expression, but nothing could be less frog-like than his voice. He was honey-tongued. Every verse he read turned into music on his lips : something midway between speech and song. It is not the only good way of reading verse, but it is the way to enchant boys ; more dramatic and less rhythmical ways can be learnt later. He first taught me the right sensuality of poetry, how it should be savoured and mouthed in solitude. Of Milton's "Thrones, Dominations, Princedoms, Virtues, Powers" he said, "That line made me happy for a week." It was not the sort of thing I had heard anyone say before. Nor had I ever met before perfect courtesy in a teacher. It had nothing to do with softness ; Smewgy could be very severe, but it was the severity of a judge, weighty and measured, without taunting —

> *He never yet ne vileyne ne sayde*
> *In all his lyf unto no maner wight.*

He had a difficult team to drive, for our form consisted partly of youngsters, New Bugs with scholarships, starting there like myself, and partly of veterans who had arrived there at the end of their slow journey up the school. He made us a unity by his good manners. He always addressed us as "gentlemen" and the possibility of behaving otherwise seemed thus to be ruled out from the beginning ; and in that room at least the distinction between fags and Bloods never raised its head. On a hot day, when he had given us permission to remove our coats, he asked our permission before removing his gown.' [7] He trusted boys to keep their own marks. With careless lavishness he would award marks above the possible maximum to a boy who gave very good answers ; but any-one else who thereupon claimed equal knowledge would be allowed to add the same number of marks to his own score. Many boys abused this trust he placed in them ; but others learnt to respect the view of life that lay behind this apparent eccentricity. C. S. Lewis continues, 'His manner was perfect : no familiarity, no hostility, no threadbare humour ; mutual respect ; decorum. "Never let us live with *amousia*", was one of his favourite maxims : *amousia*, the absence of the Muses. And he knew, as Spenser knew, that courtesy was of the Muses.

'Thus, even had he taught us nothing else, to be in Smewgy's form was to be in a measure ennobled. Amidst all the banal ambition and flashy splendours of school life he stood as a permanent reminder of things more gracious, more humane, larger and cooler. But his teaching, in the narrower sense, was equally good. He could enchant but he could also analyse. An idiom or a textual crux, once expounded by Smewgy, became clear as day. He made us feel that the scholar's demand for accuracy was not merely pedantic, still less an arbitrary moral discipline, but rather a niceness, a delicacy, to lack which argued "a gross and swainish dis-position". I began to see that the reader who misses syntactical points in a poem is missing aesthetic points as well.'

Another O.M. writes of him, 'He was a quaint old man * of owlish appearance, with round-rimmed spectacles, pop-eyes which seemed to revolve, and an odd way of sitting with one leg tucked beneath him while swinging the other to and fro. . . . When he was particularly pleased with the work

---

* Smith had come to the school in 1885 and the author of this extract is writing of a period twenty-five years later.

of any of his boys, he would send them to the headmaster "to be praised", as he put it, to the embarrassment of the headmaster, and still more of the boys themselves, whose discomfiture he rendered absolute by presenting each of them with a buttonhole of flowers, a "badge of honour" which had to be worn in Chapel. He was educated at Tonbridge and Cambridge. "Tonbridgiensis, Cantabriensior, Malverniensissimus", he would say of himself, in a sing-song crescendo, great emphasis being laid on the "issimus".' He was indeed devoted to Malvern and its boys ; and when he died during the 'flu epidemic of 1918, he left a book to each boy who had passed through his form and who was still at the school. He, too, has a room panelled in his memory.

The third master of those days, who is also today commemorated with a panelled room in the College, was Charles Toppin. He was the architect of Malvern cricket and had a tremendous influence over every boy who played the game. 'No one ever questioned or disputed "C. T.'s" opinion', writes E. R. T. Holmes in his autobiography. 'If he said anything, it *was* so. . . . I worshipped him from the moment I first met him. He was approximately fifty-five in 1919 — short and square and very leonine in countenance. He wore gold-rimmed spectacles and invariably (in the summer) a straw hat with the Free Forester ribbon round it. He walked with a stick and a limp, and normally assumed a forbidding and rather aggressive demeanour, especially when he was in cap and gown ; but when he smiled — and this was very often — it seemed that the whole School did the same, and that even the Malvern Hills and Bredon were happy, too. I would quite willingly have died for him.' Later comes an account of the Toppin manner. Holmes had taken all ten wickets for thirty-six in a match against the Shropshire Gentlemen in 1922. Toppin invited him to dinner and presented him with a ball which carried a shield recording the event, and said, 'I don't expect you'll ever do it again ; but if you do, and I'm dead and gone, come and whisper it over my grave — I'll hear you.' He continued, 'It was a great performance, and I don't want you to misunderstand what I'm going to say, d'ye see ? I'm going to tell you something now and it's this. I believe that if you ever do make your mark in the cricket world, it will be as a batsman and not as a bowler. And I think you will make a name for yourself. I may be wrong, but I doubt it. And I'm going to make this prophecy. You'll make a hundred in the 'Varsity Match, d'ye see ?' (This was almost an order.) 'I said the same thing about young Tip Foster and young Sammy Day, and they both did it. You'll do the same.' And Holmes concludes, 'And walking home to my House on that beautiful summer night, I hoped fervently that I would not let him down.' [8]

Such an incident makes one see what Donald Knight meant when he wrote, 'His method consisted in exercising his great personality rather than in employing actual technical instruction ; one felt that one was playing for *him* and for his approval, and if that was earned, it was joy and recompense indeed.' [9]

Toppin may not have given much technical instruction ; but his pupils were in no doubt as to the kind of cricket he wanted to see played. He wanted them to develop an attacking game : a good defence should be learnt afterwards. The comparatively narrow Turf at Malvern made hard strokes to the boundary past cover point particularly rewarding ; and this factor, combined with the wrist movement which the Fosters brought to the cricket field from the Rackets court, created a characterstic Malvern style with which the universities and the counties were to become very familiar. Behind all Charles Toppin's teaching of cricket, however, there lay a consuming passion, a feeling that cricket was something more than a game, that it was a way of life and a test of character by which a boy, a house, and a school could be fairly judged ; and if boys went all out for him, it was because they knew how much he cared. One of his colleagues, Douglas Berridge, who was the science master, once told the story that on an occasion when extensive alterations had to be undertaken to the Labs, he approached Toppin about using the cricket pavilion temporarily to house science classes. Toppin turned to him and said, using his nickname, 'Bewwidge-ah, I think it would be less sacrilegious to use the Chapel', — an anecdote which may sum up at least one facet of Toppin's attitude to the game.

In the class-room Toppin was more relaxed. 'His class was under less control than some', writes an O.M. 'He was fond of making little jokes, to which the class responded with a peculiar kind of applause : we would hum loudly, with our mouths tight closed. The combined effect of this would reverberate throughout the silent building, and a smile would flicker across the other class-rooms. The dignified Mr Faber * broke off in the middle of a sentence and looked down his nose with a deprecating expression, resuming his discourse only when the tempest had subsided.'

A room which, though not panelled, is named after another member of the staff is the Lyon Room, in the Music School. R. E. Lyon was a man of many parts : housemaster, Commanding Officer of the Corps and, after 1906, of the Worcestershire Volunteer Regiment, and the master in charge of the music. There had been musical activity in the school since the early days, though the programmes list pieces by Victorian composers who have long since passed into oblivion. In 1906 a more serious departure took place : Lyon launched a series of 'Classical Concerts', which meant that the effusions of obscure Victorian composers gave way to the lighter and more popular works of better-known ones. Occasionally, the programme was technically quite ambitious ; musically it was always quite safe ; and there are O.M.s with musical sensitivity who suffered deprivations and worse. One of them, referring to Lyon's organ-playing in Chapel, writes that he 'perpetrated on a helpless congregation daily improvisations of unsurpass-

---

* The Rev. H. M. Faber, housemaster of No. 1 and nephew of the first headmaster.

able hideousness'. The less sensitive either did not mind or forgave him with all their hearts. The Chapel choir always did its best for him. An O.M. recalls a succession of treble soloists 'with voices like angels, and the singing in unison was terrific !'

Musically safe, politically safer : in the Sixth Form Room the Debating Society — notwithstanding that the Chairman of the College Council was a member of Asquith's Cabinet *— kept up its solidly conservative character throughout those troubled latter years of King Edward VII's reign : Canute-like, it condemned the rise of the Labour Party, as it suddenly burst into prominence in the 1905 elections ; it withheld its confidence from the Liberal Government which followed ; in 1910 it welcomed the Osborne Judgment which prohibited trade unions from using their funds to support political parties ; and as the workers marshalled their arguments and political strength more effectively, it considered that the lower classes were over-educated (1912). When the suffragette movement was in the news, it disapproved of women having the vote (1913). Of course none of these resolutions were passed unanimously, and it cannot fairly be said that Malvern was solidly conservative ; but the outcome of a political debate could generally be foreseen. So could the result of the debate on whether the national devotion to sport was regrettable !

The other Society that flourished during those years was the Natural History Society. A body like this had been very active in the 1870s and 1880s and had then languished. Now it was revived by Henry Kempson and divided into an Archaeological, a Botanical, a Geological, an Ornithological, an Entomological, and (later) a Photographic Section. Each of these made many expeditions, especially in the summer. There were some summer terms when there was an expedition almost every week, usually to see old churches or mansions in the neighbourhood of Malvern. Sometimes the boys cycled

* Earl Beauchamp became Lord President of the Council in 1910.

there, sometimes they went by train ; and sometimes, when
M. L. Banks had taken over from Kempson, they went in
Banks' very old open car, which he used to urge uphill by
jerking himself backwards and forwards. 'Banks was easy-
going,' writes an O.M., 'and it was a simple matter to lose
him and spend a blissful afternoon eating strawberries and
cream in one of the lovely Worcestershire villages.' How
well one can imagine the pleasure of getting away from the
school grounds for an afternoon.

Apart from the extracts from English, French, and Greek
plays performed on Speech Days, there was hardly any acting
done at the school during this period ; but one of the excep-
tions was a performance by the boys of the melodrama *The
Bells* in order to raise funds for the College Mission in Canning
Town (1910). The Mission impinged more on the consciousness of Malvernians at that time than it had done before.
James was very interested in it ; and one of the masters, E. B.
Scallon, spent some time actually working and preaching in
Canning Town. The Missioner from 1905 to 1909 was G. P.
Crookenden, probably a man after James' own heart : breezy
and vigorous, possibly even a little tactless. News from the
Mission for some years took pride of place in the *Malvernian*,
immediately after the Editorials ; and the space given there
to its doings may be the excuse for some account of its work,
even if these are not strictly speaking part of the history of the
school itself. Amid a fair amount of the kind of material that
used to bore Kennedy-Cox when he was a boy at Malvern,
there are some vivid vignettes : of the Missioner going out
with a cross and two lamps, to a different street each night,
of beginning a hymn and then beginning to speak ; how at
first the audience would consist chiefly of children ; how then
presently men and women would come out of their doors and
listen ; how during a special Mission Week in 1908 the attendance at children's services rose from 400 to 800, in a parish of
7,000 people ; how the parish managed to put on a performance of *H.M.S. Pinafore* that year, and all this under conditions

of grinding poverty. In 1907 the Missioner brought a group of boys over to Malvern. They played a couple of games of football against the College boys, went to a school concert, loved their early morning swim in the swimming bath, had a rare view of the countryside from the British Camp, and attended the service in Chapel. There was a good response from Malvern boys : boys and O.M.s visited the Mission more frequently and duly wrote in the *Malvernian* of what they had seen ; the contributions to the Mission increased ; the Old Malvernian Society paid off a £500 debt on the Mission buildings and in 1910 bought the leasehold of five houses in which the missioners lived.

Crookenden left in 1909 to be succeeded by F. A. Lee, who was a very different kind of person. 'He was almost too good for our kind of work', writes Kennedy-Cox. 'Problems of vice brought to him for solution literally amazed and baffled him. He could not understand why the whole world was not good.'[10] This deficiency was made up by Lee's successor, S. G. Tinley, who became Missioner in 1911 ; and by Kennedy-Cox himself. The story of how a cheerful habitué of the West End actors' world came to give all this up as the result of a visit to the Old Bailey in search of material for a play and being shaken to the core by seeing a young sailor from the East End condemned to death for murder — this story is best read in his ebullient autobiography. He began social work at the Mission in 1908 and concentrated mainly on work with the boys. He divided them up into ten clubs, each named after a house at Malvern (in those days houses at Malvern were referred to by the housemasters' names quite as much as by their numbers), and kept them busy with football and other activities. But he was full of new ideas for the adults, too. 'They had been trying hard', he reports to the school in 1913, 'to find the right kind of service which might attract the men in particular, and they thought they had succeeded at last. It was a cinema service' (a novelty of the day) ; 'it began at nine o'clock ; the room was dark, and in this way they overcame the shyness of the men ; music was played while they were assembling, and then the bioscope was used, illustrating Old Testament, rather than New Testament, stories. They also had hymns thrown on the sheet in good, bold type.' To help the dockers fill in the time between their visit every two hours to the dock-gates to see whether the gangers had work for them that day or not, the Mission opened a hall where there was warmth, recreation, and refreshment of a non-alcoholic kind.[11] It even set up a Labour Bureau, which managed to place a very large number of unemployed. Perhaps it was not an exaggeration when Kennedy-Cox told the school in 1914 that its Mission probably touched some 2,000 people in the 7,000 strong parish. At midnight on New Year's Eve of 1912 the crowd in the little corrugated iron church was so dense that the Missioner was quite unable to get into the pulpit and had to preach from the altar steps.

That little church would clearly not do much longer — quite apart from the occasional inconvenience of having some little devils throw cascades of stones on to the corrugated roof during services [12] and the fact that the white-painted pebbles which had been stuck on a piece of scarlet flannel to form the words 'Holy, Holy, Holy !' were beginning to fall off so that 'the words gradually seemed to represent, to the uninitiated, Hebrew or some other strange language'.[13] It was decided in 1911 to start raising the £7,000 which would be needed for a brick church. In the Christmas holidays of 1912/13, Malvern boys collected £254 towards that sum. They certainly were made aware of the problems that face a growing congregation.

The school, too, was growing during a good part of James' Headmastership. When he came there were 417 boys at the College, and during his time numbers reached a maximum of 509. Such increases inevitably mean more buildings and financial problems until they are paid for. The last of the houses, No. 9, had its origins in 1897, when E. C. Bullock was allowed to turn the house which he had rented, 'Cranhill', into a boarding-house. This soon proved too small and in 1899 'Malvernbury', where, it will be remembered, No. 6 had started its existence, was again rented from Dyson Perrins to accommodate No. 9. But in the long run, rented accommodation was hardly a satisfactory solution ; and when Roslin House came onto the market in 1901, the Council began to negotiate for it. The negotiations broke down, and the Council decided instead to build another house below No. 5, where the Gym stands today. But just at that time it became necessary to renew the antiquated heating system of the College (1902) ;* the Council decided to postpone building operations ; and before they could take them up again, Bullock bought Roslin House himself and enlarged it with a boys' wing. The Council promised to buy it from him when he should leave it ; and so in 1903 No. 9 finally moved into its present quarters.

In the same year Lyon bought the house which he had previously rented, and again the Council promised to buy it off him when he should leave it, so that No. 7 also now effectively belonged to the College. There remained No. 8. This, it will be remembered, had started in 'Malvernhurst'. From there it moved into 'Malvernbury' when Bullock vacated it in 1903. Then in 1906, when the death of C. D. Barker, a member of the College Council, left Radnor House vacant, the Council borrowed the money to buy and enlarge the house, and C. T. Salisbury moved his boys into the present accommodation.† The grounds of Radnor House, which the College bought at the same time, stretched right down to No. 3, and in this way much building land was acquired which was to be put to full use a generation later.

The Council also wanted to buy School House from Earl Beauchamp instead of continuing to rent it ; but the Earl wanted £12,000 for it and the Council was willing to pay

---

* Electricity was installed in 1909.

† 'Malvernbury', having housed successively Nos. 6, 8 and 9, was soon afterwards pulled down. The Old Peoples' Home in Abbey Road, though also called 'Malvernbury', is a newer building on the same site.

only £11,000 ; so nothing came of these negotiations (1899) : just how regrettably emerged only later.

Meanwhile, the work on the new chapel was continued. Gray had undertaken to raise the money for it ; but with his early retirement, the Council felt obliged to pay the difference (£1,423) between the money collected and the cost of the chapel itself. In 1899 the new chapel was opened. Its lines are remarkably pure for the period. The inspiration is Perpendicular rather than Decorated or Early Gothic, and it has none of the gloom of many Victorian school chapels. It is a little on the severe side even today and was even barer when it was opened. The low aisle did not yet break up the south wall and enrich it with its shadows ; the fine reredos was put up only later in James' Headmastership ; the statues in it followed, and the plain glass in the windows was gradually replaced by stained glass.* The O.M. Society gave the organ. Within eight years of being opened, the new chapel was too small to take the growing numbers in the school, and in 1908 C. J. Blomfield, the son of Sir Arthur who had recently died, designed the south aisle irreverently known to Malvernians as 'the rabbit hutches'. The money for this was raised by donations. The chapel could now seat 570, still too small for the Sundays when there are many parents : at Speech Day weekend and at Confirmation there usually have to be two services to accommodate the numbers.

The old chapel was now turned into three class-rooms, a music room, and a museum for the ever-growing collection of geological specimens and other items relating to natural and ancient history.

There were other additions and alterations to the school buildings. The Sanatorium was enlarged in 1902. James

---

* Some of these windows are memorial ones : the great East window commemorates the Malvernians who were killed in the Boer War ; on the north side are windows in memory of Faber, Grundy, James, and Foster ; one on the south side in memory of Canon Estridge, the first housemaster of No. 4. There is also on the south side a window given by the mothers of Malvernians. Details of the other windows and of the general scheme can be found in Appendix D.

introduced Civil Engineering into the syllabus and an Engineering School was built by the Council in 1902. It had a good start; but later on pupils fell off, and it never really paid its way. The biggest project was the building by the O.M. Society, at a cost of £11,000, of a second Rackets Court and of the present Gymnasium bloc, complete with Lodge, School Shop, and Fives Courts in 1903. The old gymnasium was converted into an Armoury and Science class-rooms. Finally, a small-bore rifle range was built in 1907.

The help given by the O.M. Society in those years was not confined to financing building operations. In 1903 it took up the suggestion of its Chairman, Cecil Braithwaite, that it should set itself the most important task of acquiring by purchase or gift the shares of the College.★ By 1912 it had acquired 492 of the 574 shares.

The fact that Old Malvernians were now such substantial shareholders meant in due course that they were more heavily represented on the governing bodies of the school. In 1905, the vacancy on the Council caused by the death of the Chairman, G. E. Martin, was filled by W. H. Hadow, the distinguished musicologist, later Vice-Chancellor of Sheffield University and Chairman of the Committee which in 1926 produced the Hadow Report on Religious Education. He was the first O.M. on the Council. When C. D. Barker died in 1906, he too was replaced by an O.M., John Lea-Smith. In 1908 the O.M. Society transferred its shares to the names of twenty-four of its members, which entitled them to attend the Annual General Meetings ; and the idea arose that the Council of the College might be entirely re-modelled, to reflect the importance not only of the Old Malvernian Society, but also of the Universities and of the Army.

The new Constitution came into force in 1912. Henceforward the College Council was made up of three members nominated by the Lords-Lieutenant of Worcestershire,

★ Braithwaite had already given to the Society the fifteen shares he held, this being but one of his benefactions to Malvern.

Gloucestershire, and Herefordshire respectively, two nominated by the Vice-Chancellors of Oxford and Cambridge respectively, one nominated by the Army Council, one nominated by the Headmaster and the Assistant Masters, six Old Malvernians, two co-opted clergy of the Church of England, and up to eleven other members. The distinguished names on the new Council show the reputation that Malvern College had with the outside world. They included Stanley Baldwin, M.P. ; the Vice-Provost of King's College, Cambridge ; the Chichele Professor of History at Oxford ; the Dean of St. Paul's ; and the Bishop of Barking.

Such a Council could obviously not be expected to spend as much time as the old Council had done on minor items of repair to buildings and grounds, and this kind of business was now transferred to a Works and Finance Sub-Committee, to which a Bursar was appointed. In the course of the next half-century this Committee was destined to deal with formidable legal and financial problems, among them the debenture consolidation in 1919, the Royal Charter ten years later, the impact of the Depression in the thirties, and the two evacuations in the Second World War. The school owes a very great debt to the members of this Committee and particularly to their Chairmen, C. Stewart Cox (1912 to 1932), S. P. Richardson (1932 to 1941), the ninth Viscount Cobham (1941 to 1949), Sir Reginald Hills (1949 to 1956), and J. A. Deed (since 1956), who were unsparing in putting their time and experience at the disposal of the College.

At the time when the new Constitution had first been suggested by James in 1910, the finances of the College were suffering less from the burdens of the past than they ever had before. The profit margin was so small, however, that a fall in the number of boys would immediately put a serious strain on the school's finances ; and towards the end of James' Headmastership, numbers did decline. When he left, they were down to 456, fifty-three fewer than at the peak in 1908 ; and during his last three years of office, the College income fell short of its expenditure, something that had not happened for a quarter of a century. James gave the following explanation for this decline on Speech Day of 1912 :

'It is not so much that fewer boys come to the school as that some boys are taken away earlier than used to be the case. Some parents are made nervous by the financial schemes associated with the name of Mr. Lloyd George. (Hear, hear.) I am no politician, mind you, and I am not talking about politics — but, no question about it, there has been a great deal of uneasiness in the upper and upper-middle classes from which we draw our boys, as to the hen-roost which may next be attacked. . . . And then there is the lowering of the age of entry for the Army which may have had its effects.'

There were other reasons too, judging by the fact that there was a much greater fall in some houses than in others. No. 5, for example, suffered a particularly severe decline when Foster retired from his housemastership in 1908 and James decided on that occasion to move Toppin, his large family and his boys from the comparatively small house on the north side of the grounds into Foster's old house, while Foster's boys, under their new bachelor housemaster, L. S. Milward, moved across into the house that Toppin vacated.

And then there may have been matters that could hardly have been mentioned at Speech Day. There is no doubt that some parents were withdrawing their sons as the result of discovering that the moral tone was suffering from what one writer about the period calls 'the evils of a monastic institution'. C. S. Lewis has described their extent in his autobiography * and how gossip about who had connections with whom took second place only to talk about games. Entries in the school prefects' minute book for 1910, 1911, and 1912 bear this out, though scarcely with as much frankness as C. S. Lewis' account. The concept of immorality ranged from smoking through swearing and lewd talk to 'meeting and

* *Surprised by Joy.* The school is thinly disguised under the name of Wyvern.

talking to girls on Sundays' (for which offence two house-prefects were degraded), spreading scandal, and 'disgusting behaviour'. Much to the point is the remark of a Head of School that 'during the holidays he had heard of people who had refused to send their sons to Malvern because of the bad language and filthy talk which went on there'.

How to eradicate this kind of trouble, especially when it is widespread, is a problem that has faced other headmasters besides James, and at other schools and at other times. One may take it that James expelled any boy against whom he had evidence ; and indeed scarcely a term went by during his headmastership when he did not report one or more expulsions to the Council. Sometimes the reason is given in the minutes, 'for immorality', 'for pilfering' ; at other times it was 'for reasons deemed sufficient by the Council'. We need not necessarily put the worst construction on this elastic phrase. James tells us in his autobiography that he expelled boys for persistent idleness,[14] and an O.M. of the period writes of other boys who were expelled for a variety of offences. The Irish earl who sent a donkey up the aisle of the Chapel during the service and who was in the habit of carrying a revolver, 'loading one chamber only, rushing into your study, and then firing off (if that is the right word) all the others at you, so that your life depended on his counting accurately'[15] was not asked to leave ; but the picaresque adventures of one who was expelled have been enshrined in fiction. The author, Michael Arlen, was at Malvern under a different name,* a new boy then, on whom the escapade of his senior obviously made an indelible impression. The passage in his novel *Piracy* is not quite accurate in all details ; but it is so entertaining that it may perhaps be set down here, with footnotes, based on the reminiscences of a master of that time, to indicate the historical truth :

'There were rumours, new rumours every morning, delightful and outrageous rumours, so that the lumps in the

* D. Kouyoumdjian.

porridge were swallowed without comment and the fish-cakes were eaten without contumely. The masters looked un-usually stern, but it was the sternness of thought rather than of discipline. Coll Prees went about with smiles gravely repressed and an air of being more than usually responsible for everything. House Prees and Bloods (indescribable beings, neither Prefect nor Inferior, amazing centaurs, not divine but certainly not human — just Bloods) were everywhere to be seen in earnest colloquy. For the matter was that there was some sort of night-prowler about the school grounds. It would have been almost bearable if the night-prowler had prowled only about the grounds, but he prowled into the Houses, he prowled actually into the Housemasters' sides of the Houses ; he prowled into their studies, he sat on their chairs, he read their books, he drank their port, he tested their barley water, he smoked their cigars, he left a neat little bit of Greek verse on their desks to thank them for the same * — and then, as it were for a joke, he bolted the windows from the inside, locked the doors from the outside, and left the keys in such an obvious place that no one ever found them until new ones had been made. And this went on, once or twice a week, for more than a month ! Watch was kept, police were stationed about the grounds (for weeks any strange face about the school grounds was held to be that of a "plain clothes man — and jolly plain at that !") and the Coll Prees were called upon to keep night watch over the House where each held dominion. . . . Then there was a memorable night when the night prowler was chased. Two Coll Prees and Mr. Sandys, of the Lower Fifth and the Hampshire Eleven, † were patrolling the borders of the Senior Turf, about which lie the main houses of Manton in the form of a horse-shoe.

---

* He did nothing as foolish as to provide his victims with specimens of his handwriting. He left behind or sent through the post notes laboriously written in pin-pricks. James' note read, 'We think your cigars delicious and hope your desk is not much hurt'.

† This was probably R. B. Porch, who played for Somerset. In fact the chase was made by a detective.

Suddenly, just ahead of them, was seen a moving dark thing. They leapt. It ran. They chased, but the dark thing hurtled down the slope from the path to the flat darkness of the Senior Turf. "He's got running shorts," grumbled Mr. Sandys, who was in a dinner-jacket. "And gym-shoes," grunted Mr. Sandys. Then came a laugh behind them, and again they leapt. But the dark thing grew darker and disappeared into the labyrinth of buildings made by the gymnasium, the gates, racket-courts, and House No. 6. "Blast!" said Mr. Sandys, and gave up. The Coll Prees had given up long before.*

'Of course the night prowler was caught in the end . . .' and from this point onwards Arlen's account becomes purely fictional. In fact, a search in houses during chapel one Sunday morning led to the discovery of torch, jemmy, and a photograph of the boy in burglar's costume in his locker.

The asides in Arlen's account allow one to conclude that, like C. S. Lewis, he was among those Malvernians who looked at the life of a Malvern schoolboy with a distinctly critical eye. This emerges also from other passages in the novel, like this comment on the hierarchy among the boys : 'The difference between a College Prefect and a House Prefect is that a Coll Pree can do what he likes everywhere, and a House Pree can do what he likes in his House. Inferiors can do what they like in their studies, more or less. Fags can't do what they like anywhere.' C. S. Lewis, who disliked Malvern so much that he was taken away at the end of his first year, goes into more

---

* What really happened was even more amusing. The boy almost stepped into the arms of the detective, who was standing by the Armoury ; but he 'slipped past him and ran into the darkness and along the Senior Bank up to half-way, the detective after him. Having a good lead, he then turned left, straight down the bank, and made for the centre of the Senior, where in those days, because horses often got into the grounds at night, the match wickets square was surrounded by barbed wire. He reckoned that, even if his pursuer had seen him turn down the bank, the barbed wire would give him a good start if he had to go on to the Junior. Once there, he lay down flat and waited, but the detective had lost him from the start. I like the idea of the centre of the Senior Turf being the best hiding place for a fugitive !'

details in his autobiography. He describes at length the aristocracy of the 'Bloods', whose most important qualification is athletic prowess, ruling at the top of a pyramid of which the fags formed the exploited base. 'Different schools have different kinds of fagging', he writes. 'At some of them, individual Bloods have individual fags. This is the system most often depicted in school stories ; it is sometimes represented as — and for all I know, sometimes really is — a fruitful relation as of knight and squire, in which service on the one part is rewarded by some degree of countenance and protection on the other. But whatever its merits may be, we never experienced them at Wyvern. Fagging was with us as impersonal as the labour-market in Victorian England. . . . All boys under a certain seniority constituted a labour pool, the common property of all the Bloods.★ When a Blood wanted his O.T.C. kit brushed and polished, or his boots cleaned, or his study "done out", or his tea made, he shouted. We all came running, and of course the Blood gave the work to the boy he most disliked.' †

But the majority of boys probably took the hierarchy in their stride and approved of it even when they were still at the bottom. Here is an account from a near-contemporary of C. S. Lewis' :

'It was a good life at Malvern in those days. . . . It was the *fairness* of everything that, above all, appealed to me. There was no bullying, the prefects saw to that ; if a couple of boys were caught fighting, the scrap was broken up, and they had it out, fairly, in the reading room the same evening, with boxing gloves and a referee, with the rest of the house as

★ This word should at least read 'house-prefect' in the context. Bloods (the leading games players) were not necessarily prefects, though of course many of them were. Only prefects had fags.
† The fagging system has been modified since then. It is no longer impersonal : a house-prefect will have two or three 'personal fags' attached to him who do personal services like shoe-cleaning for him. The fag-call is used when a more general chore has to be done, and the work is given to the boy who arrives last on the scene in response to the call. For it to be given to the boy the prefect most disliked will have been comparatively rare even in C. S. Lewis' time.

spectators. Plenty of caning went on, but it was fair. There was almost a tariff for it : for example, cutting a game produced a warning the first time, three strokes the second, and six of the best for subsequent offences. Thus you knew what you were in for, and, when the punishment was over, the misdeed was forgotten.'

Perhaps a book on an English public school should take the hierarchy and the fagging system for granted. Certainly the majority of Malvernians both then and now do so, even when they are at the bottom of the school, and will be quite cheerful and happy under circumstances under which a middle-class adult would be extremely unhappy, fagging quite apart : one need only think of the lack of privacy of any kind at a boarding school.* Yet a minority of boys, and those the more sensitive, will not be happy ; and the argument often advanced that this minority consists solely of people who would be misfits anywhere, of natural outsiders or born rebels, is simply not true. There are some places into which it is more difficult to fit than others, and there are some times which are harder than others. There seems little doubt that to have been at Malvern just before the First World War *as one of the minority* was to have been at a harsh place at a harsh time. A military O.M., who can write that what he liked most about Malvern at this time was 'the wonderful esprit de corps *throughout the Coll.*' (my italics), writes at the same time that a new boy, 'provided he realized for the first year that he was the lowest form of life in the Coll, *could* lead a quiet life, free from trouble' (his italics), and that if the Head of House did

---

* Although in those days, unlike today, all the dormitories had cubicles, 'in my house the one opportunity for privacy that I think is general elsewhere was denied, as the lavatories had not been equipped with doors. Six latrines stood in a row in an ill-favoured pent-house in the yard, exposed to the view from in front, and with only a thin partition between them. To the average new boy, the victim of taboo from waist to knees, . . . it was not a re-assuring arrangement.' (Derek Verschoyle on Malvern in the 1920s.) In another house at that time, however, the lavatories in the yard did have doors, and it was the privilege of those who had been there three years to keep them *open*. It was a chilly business in the winter and at such times prefects in one house would send fags to warm the seats by prior occupation.

not exert himself, 'House Prefects could be unbearable to inferiors'.

It was of course a harsh time in England as a whole during those years. The Boer War and then the growing tensions in Europe, almost more than the social stresses at home, had their effects on the school. The excitement caused by the Boer War at school was understandable enough. Of the 153 Old Malvernians who are known to have fought in South Africa, several sent reports home to the *Malvernian*, which carried an article from the front in almost every issue. When Ladysmith was relieved, the Headmaster sent the under-porter round the class-rooms with the news ; and four months later, when the relief of Mafeking became known, the whole school, led by B. S. Foster (whose brother W. L. Foster was one of those fighting in South Africa), broke bounds and rushed 'up Town' ('for what purpose I never discovered', writes the O.M. who sent this piece of information) ; and a fireworks display was held when the news arrived that Pretoria had been captured. Seventeen Old Malvernians were killed in that war : they are commemorated in the East window of the chapel. D. R. Younger was one of the two O.M.s to be awarded a posthumous Victoria Cross. (The other was Major Kenneth Muir, during the Korean War in 1950.)

England was never the same after the Boer War. The nation felt humiliated by the length of time it had taken to overcome the small Boer republics and alarmed by the hostile chorus from the other countries of Europe. 'Splendid Isolation' in foreign affairs looked less splendid. England began to look round for friends and found that in the process she became involved in the tensions that were building up for the First World War.

James personally saw to it that the school should be aware of these things. Just as he protested every Speech Day that he did not want games to be a religion, so he reiterated year after year that he was no militarist. But he was at any rate drawn to matters military. He had immensely enjoyed commanding the Eton Corps,* and an O.M. writes, 'One would not have taken him for a parson. He would have made an admirable divisional general or perhaps a Corps Commander'. In any case, the Malvern Corps got ceaseless encouragement at his hands.

When James came, it was still an Artillery Corps. In 1888 an Army Directive had ordered schools to dispense with Artillery ; but pleas from Malvern to be exempted from this order were successful. For the next twenty years it was the only school artillery corps in the country. As such it marched past at the head of the public schools column on the occasions when the Field Day took place at Aldershot. It was equipped with four nine-pounder, muzzle-loading, horse-drawn field pieces. These guns could be a hazard. One field-day at Marlborough in 1895 the horses took fright and started to bolt, dragging the guns through the ranks of the contingent and seriously injuring one of the gunners. By 1903 the field pieces were considered so antiquated and liable to blow the gunners to bits that, to the great indignation of the Corps, the War Office telegraphed that the guns must not be fired at the Marlborough Field Day, and they stayed behind at Malvern. In 1908 the Volunteer Regiments were merged in the Territorial Force, and on that occasion the Cadet Corps of the Public Schools were embodied as contingents of the Junior Division of the Officers' Training Corps (O.T.C.), and despite renewed protests and pleas, the War Office decided that there was no place for artillery in the schools under the new dispensation.

Under the circumstances, it was natural that more attention should be paid to Rifle Shooting, especially as the Volunteer

* He writes as following about his reasons for applying for the Headmastership of Malvern : 'There was the possibility of getting into a groove and staying there, of becoming mechanical and perhaps lazy. I could not expect to command the Corps indefinitely ; I was getting near the end of my tether as a football player, and should soon lose touch with the boys in active games.' (*Seventy Years*, p. 134.)

Rifle Club movement had been a strongly established feature
of other public schools since the 1880s.[16] In 1906 James had
set on foot plans to build a rifle range, and from that time
onwards not a Speech Day passed without boys being urged
by the Headmaster to learn rifle shooting. 'There is nothing
of what is called militarism in this project,' he said in 1906 ;
'I am convinced that for self-preservation our country must
have men trained to shoot and men of sound physical development, and that it is the duty of the public schools to take their
part — and that a leading part — in such training. For, in
case of need, where are the officers of a home defence to come
from if not from the class of men who have been educated at
the great public schools ? Training of the kind we hope to
give is in my opinion the cheapest and most practical form of
national insurance. (Applause.)' In 1907 he assured parents
that there would be no compulsion on a boy to join the Corps :
'Compulsion is foreign to the very nature of Volunteering' ;
yet there was training in rifle shooting for every boy ; in
1911, when the Corps again went to Windsor for the Corona-
tion Review of George V, the Malvern Corps was the third
biggest in the country ; and in 1913, 435 out of the 461 boys
in the school were members of the O.T.C. In 1912, the
Malvernian printed a letter from Field-Marshal Lord Roberts,
appealing to boys who were about to leave to join the Army.
'As you know,' ended the letter, 'some of our fellow-country-
men across the seas have already adopted the principle that it
is the duty of every man to be trained in the use of arms ;
believe me, boys, you can give no greater service to your
country than by doing your utmost to procure the adoption
of the same noble principle in the Motherland.'

All this, against the background of the steadily worsening
international situation, had its effect. A small symptom was
that in 1902 the Debating Society opposed conscription and in
1911 supported it. More to the point was the very large
number of Old Malvernians who did join the Regular Army.
H. W. Smith, who gave up charge of the Grundy Library in

1907 and then devoted his spare time to the labour of love of collecting news about the doings of Old Malvernians, found 380 O.M.s on the Army Active List in 1909 ; there is no record of the number in the Territorial Army. Of course many Malvernians had made the Army their career ever since the school was founded and especially after Grundy had started the Army Class in 1888 ; but the tempo of enlistment certainly quickened at about this time. Today we remember the frightful slaughter of England's young manhood in the First World War, and one feels the terrible irony of that word 'Applause' from parents who were to lose their sons and from boys who were to lay down their lives. Yet the danger of war was real ; the need for men, at a time when England alone among the great nations had no conscription, was urgent ; and if it came to a war, no one then knew of a way of winning which did not depend on the willingness of trained young men to fight for their country. No one, it must be added, thought that the war would be so different in kind from earlier wars. When, in 1904, on an inspection of the Malvern Corps, Lieutenant-General Sir John French said that 'doubtless he was speaking to several who would one day find themselves leading men in actual war', he could have had little idea of the dreadful extent to which his prophecy was to become true. Certainly no one anticipated the appalling casualty lists, and many people really thought that the number of men who could fire a rifle efficiently could well be as decisive a factor on the battlefields of Europe as it had been on those of South Africa. In military as in social affairs, the old order was changing rapidly.

And the old order was changing too at Malvern, at least as far as personnel was concerned. The death in 1910 of the first headmaster, Canon Faber, was followed in 1911 by that of his successor, Canon Cruttwell. Frederick Prosser, who had been the School Porter since 1869, retired in 1906, his pink and pitted face now framed with white hair and beard. George Arber, who had come as a cricket professional in 1869, retired at the same time. After he had given up active cricket in 1887,* he had continued work as a groundsman and had been owner of the first school shop in Poolend Road, now No. 1, The Lees. He had also set up as a builder and, employed by Holcombe Ingleby (Member of Parliament, poet, and an O.M. who hymned his school in nostalgic Victorian verse), he built the semicircle of houses that today stand in The Lees. Anyone who looks at The Lees today can see that he improved as he went round ! He was generally known as 'G' and was much liked.

Then there was a regular exodus of housemasters in these years, some of whom had held their houses for many, many years. In 1912 J. N. Swann gave up No. 2 after twenty-two years and the Rev. T. Spear left No. 3 after thirty-five years. In 1913 the Rev. H. M. Faber retired from No. 1 after twenty-six years, and C. T. Salisbury gave up No. 8 after a mere eighteen years. But the record for long tenure was held by the Rev. Henry Foster, 'the Old Man', now so deaf that his class sat round the table at which he presided. He retired from No. 5 in 1908, having run this house for thirty-seven years, and became Second Master. A good deal has been said about his sons in the preceding pages — his last two sons fittingly won the Public School Rackets Competition just before he gave up the House. Of his pride in his sons there can be little doubt — two of them were Heads of School and three others Heads of House — and of his wife's pride in them there is today a memorial on the Terrace from which cricket on the Senior Turf is watched : the bench from which she saw her sons win glories on the pitch below is inscribed 'Mrs Foster sat here'. The Fosters also had three daughters. Two of them married Malvern housemasters,† and all three of them

---

* 'He was a player of the old-fashioned school, who could find no value in modern developments and it is doubtful whether he was a great coach', writes Toppin. 'His "Come out to them, Sir", was heard too frequently. But he was a fine character, sturdy and independent to a degree, and honest as the day.' (*Malvern College Register*, II, p. xxiii.)

† Jessie Foster married W. Greenstock ; and Mabel Foster married E. C. Bullock : she died four years later, aged only twenty-seven.

were good games players. James writes of Jessie : 'She was a good bowler and would have had a capital chance of getting into any school eleven on her merits'.

One more fact and then we have done with this legendary family. In 1909 G. N. Foster went out to India, where he became Secretary to H.H. the Jam Sahib of Nawanagar, better known in England as Ranjitsinhji, the Prince of Cricket, who had been 'Champion Batsman' for All England in 1895 and again in 1900. In the course of time the Jam Sahib sent four of his nephews to Malvern, two of whom duly played in the Cricket Eleven and later held high positions in India, one as Commander-in-Chief and the other as Deputy Defence Minister. In 1912 their uncle, who had been appointed to the Council two years before, came to Malvern to give away the prizes at the Speech Day ceremony for which Stanley Baldwin was in the Chair. In his speech on that occasion, Ranjitsinhji explained that the reason he had sent his nephews to Malvern was not only because he greatly admired the prowess of the Fosters and the Days in games, but also because they had previously been at a school in India entirely for the sons and relations of the ruling princes of that country. He had found that their early training there had not altogether tallied with his ideas of work : they had too much liberty, they were pampered too much, they had too many servants, and he thought the best thing for the development of their character was to send them to a public school in England. He freely confessed that he was a great admirer of the English character and trusted that he had imbued some good from the English training he had received. Considering that the newspapers had been full of reports of unrest in India at about this time (the Jam Sahib referred to them as 'the misdeeds of a fanatical few'), it did his audience good to hear this speech ; and James only expressed what they all felt when, after complimenting his guest on his sixty-ninth century in first-class cricket achieved only the week before, he added, 'Speaking of more serious things, I am convinced that one great guarantee of the stability

of our Indian Empire is to be found in the existence of independent reigning princes, who, like you, sir, understand us
English people, sympathize with our English ways, and take
part in our English life.'

Malvernians were in fact deeply committed in India. In
1909 H. W. Smith collected the names of forty-eight O.M.s
who were in the government service in India, and there will
have been many others who were there in an unofficial capacity.
One of these (A. P. Collett), who was acting as a magistrate
at Benares, received a petition from an Indian which ended
with the pious prophecy, 'God shall give you the degree of
Lord Governor General'. This particular prophecy was not
fulfilled ; but it is a fact that Malvern has produced more men
of distinction in Colonial Administration than in any other
field.* The record begins with Sir Hugh Barnes, who entered
Malvern when the school was only one year old and who
became Governor of Burma,† and it ends with men as diverse
in outlook as Sir Godfrey Huggins, who took the title of Lord
Malvern on relinquishing his Premiership of Southern Rhodesia
(1933 to 1956), ‡ and Sir Andrew Cohen, Governor of Uganda
from 1952 to 1957. In between, there are men who have
presided over the destinies of Mauritius, Kenya, Gambia,
British Guiana, and Jamaica (Sir Edward Denham) ; the
Seychelles and the Leeward Islands (the Hon. Eustace Edward
Twisleton-Wykeham-Fiennes) ; the Punjab (Sir Geoffrey de
Montmorency) ; Madras (Sir Geoffrey Bracken) ; Palestine,
Aden, Tanganyika, and the Sudan (Sir Stewart Symes) ;
Bengal, and Assam (Sir Robert Reid). Most of these O.M.s
reached their high positions later than the period now under
discussion ; but Sir Hugh Barnes had become Governor of
Burma in 1903 and old Henry Foster could remember him
as a boy at the school.

The retirement of so many housemasters enabled James to

* On the Victorian Public Schools and Imperialism, see E. C. Mack,
Public Schools and British Opinion, 1780–1860, pp. 291-292.
† He gave away prizes on the Speech Day of 1907.
‡ He gave away prizes on the Speech Day of 1953.

make some changes in their status. He had never been happy with the enormous power the housemasters had when he first came to Malvern. In his autobiography he writes, 'When I came, I found that there were also housemasters' meetings at which, as in a sort of Cabinet, discussions took place on important matters, and resolutions were actually passed and recorded : it might even happen that the Headmaster might be outvoted. These meetings I abolished at once, and I did not permit voting at the ordinary masters' meetings. But of course I allowed the freest expression of opinion from all, though the responsibility of decision was mine and mine alone.' [17]

Clearly the unlimited tenure of houses could be an enormous obstacle to change of any sort and must have been profoundly discouraging to the younger men on the staff, though on the whole there was a far smaller turn-over of young masters than there is in most schools nowadays. One of the masters of that period recalls that in 1914, when he had been teaching at Malvern for ten years and was aged thirty-nine, he was only three or four from the bottom of the staff !

As it became clear to James that the régime of the old housemasters would not last much longer, he determined that their successors should have a more limited tenure ; and in 1907, before any of these retirements took place, it was decided by the Council that the maximum tenure should in the normal course of events be fifteen years. On the retirement of Salisbury, another important principle was embodied in the Council minutes, namely that the headmaster was not bound to appoint to a vacant housemastership the next man in order of seniority.

These changes came late in James' headmastership and did not have their full effect for some time. They do not seriously mitigate the impression that in his last few years the school was getting a little set in its ways ; and James, who had decided when he first came to Malvern that about fifteen years ought to be the limit of his own tenure of office,* was clearly right to adhere to this decision. 'I was nearly fifty-nine, not too old to do some active work if I could find it,† but not quite as fresh as I had been — and a schoolmaster ought to be fresh.' He prolonged his tenure a little beyond the fifteen years mainly because he wanted to see the new Constitution of the College in working order. 'But in the autumn of 1913 I sent in my resignation, to take effect at Easter 1914. I chose Easter because I thought that my successor would find the machine running smoothly in the last term of the school year, would be able to see what changes he would like to make, and would have the long summer holidays in which to work them out.'

In these long summer holidays, the First World War broke out.

---

* 'It seemed to me, from what I had seen elsewhere, that after that time a change would be desirable both for the school and for the man.' (*Seventy Years*, p. 188.)

† James actually retired to Bembridge, on the Isle of Wight. When the war came, there was a remarkable series of coincidences. First he found that the brigade of the Worcestershire Territorial Artillery under E. C. Bullock, the housemaster of No. 9, was stationed on the island, and for some time he acted as its chaplain. He raised and commanded a company of Volunteers in Bembridge and in 1915 he took up a chaplaincy with the 2nd South Midland Brigade of the Territorial Artillery. This brigade was commanded by none other than Col. Lyon, who had raised it himself and had about a dozen O.M.s and the assistant school doctor (Dr. Mackie) among his officers. 'My lot could not possibly have fallen in happier lines', writes James. When the Brigade was posted overseas — it later fought in the Battle of the Somme — James, then aged sixty, was not allowed to go with them ; but he remained a chaplain to the forces for the remainder of the war.

CHAPTER VII

The Headmastership of F. S. Preston
1914–1937

JAMES had only been in Deacon's Orders when he was appointed headmaster ; and in accordance with the then requirements of the Constitution, he had taken Priest's Orders within three months of his appointment. But in 1912 the clause requiring the headmaster to be a clergyman was removed from the Constitution ; and F. S. Preston was the first lay headmaster in the history of the College.* He had been a boy and later a housemaster at Marlborough ; and at Pembroke College, Cambridge, he had been a distinguished classical scholar. Other headmasters of Malvern have matched him in erudition ; but few have thought as deeply about the nature of the good life and the kind of education that will best help to make boys realize it. It is true that Preston's predecessors had not been called upon to make the same searching analysis. The traditional way in which the public school system worked began to be questioned soon after the turn of the century ; but it was not until after the First World War that this criticism assumed considerable proportions.

As one would expect, the reactions of public school men to such criticisms varied. Some were entirely impervious to them ; some saw weaknesses that certainly stood in need of correction ; others again wanted a drastic break with the spirit of the past. Preston belonged to the second category. Believing that the public schools must continue to provide

---

* He was, however, an active lay preacher, addressing nonconformist as well as Anglican congregations ; and he was for over thirty years an active member of the Church Assembly.

leadership, he strove on the one hand to create a balanced atmosphere in which respect for games did not swamp respect for things of the mind, whilst on the other he set his face against the growing tendency to regard education as a preparation for a job rather than as a preparation for life. He had the fastidious outlook of a natural aristocrat. The despoliation of beauty, whether of language or of landscape, was abhorrent to him ; with materialism in any form he was totally out of sympathy ; and he disliked most of the cultural developments of his time. But with all that he showed flexibility in widening the concept of education beyond the primarily classical framework he found when he came to Malvern and in giving to all the modern studies a great deal more scope than they had had hitherto.

Preston hardly had time to introduce any changes before the First World War broke out. The impact on the school was immediate. A number of the staff joined up at once. They included the two housemasters who were already Colonels in the Territorial Army, Lyon and Bullock. In the next twelve months middle-aged men were accepted as volunteers ; and in 1916 conscription made further inroads on the staff.

The work of the Corps assumed a new urgency. It now drilled twice a week, and there was the occasional night-operation which thrilled the boys who were soon to have night operations in real earnest. The school had to recommend boys for the Officers Training Units, and since a very large number of boys wanted to volunteer at the first possible moment, they trained with a will. Especially at the beginning of the war, a large number of senior boys left for the Army as soon as they had reached volunteering age. The numbers in the school dropped from 456 in the summer of 1914 to 400 in the summer of 1915 ; and since the intake continued to be normal, early leaving accounts for almost the whole of that drop. On Speech Day of 1915, Preston urged that some boys were really not fit to leave quite so soon. 'If we were to appeal to the members of the School, they would say they were all fit ; and parents may be certain that, speaking for the house-masters and myself, there is no desire to check the patriotism or enthusiasm of any boy whom we realize to be a possible officer in the near future. However, without wishing to hurt anybody's feelings, there are a certain number of patriots in the School who are hardly possible officers in the near future, and I cannot but advise parents to be guided to a certain extent by the opinion of a boy's housemaster. I will quote something I read the other day, written by one official to another : "Large numbers of young men — almost boys — have entered the Army before they have been physically or morally ripe for the demands of a campaign. They have thereby ruined their lives without helping their country. The great using up of the educated part of the youth of a country involves the danger of a decline in the intellectual activity of a people in all spheres of life." I do not say I agree with that. You prob-ably do not suspect its origin. It was written by the Prussian Minister of War to the Prussian Minister of Education. We can occasionally learn something even from a German, and the point I would wish to make is that age is no criterion of a boy's physical or moral ripeness for a campaign. A sense of responsibility is needed ; a certain standard of intelligence is required ; and it would be fatal — especially if we are faced with a long war — to mar a great deal of good material by taking it too young. (Applause.) Apart from that, I agree that those who are fit should certainly go.'

Statistics indicate that these words had some effect ; but just before conscription was introduced, 1,900 O.M.s were known to be serving in the Forces, and 150 had already lost their lives.

At school, there were considerable problems. There was the difficulty of replacing the staff who had joined up. Properly qualified substitutes were hardly obtainable. Old men came out of retirement to help. Medically unfit men joined the staff. At one time Mathematics was taught in the Sixth Form by the wife of a solicitor who had been called up, and French by a lady whose finishing school in Paris had closed down. Preston had only just come, and was not yet endowed with that invaluable mystique by virtue of which a headmaster can often work miracles ; and besides, the constant reorganization required by the departure of one member of the staff after another imposed such a strain on him that he had to take a term off on medical advice.

Meanwhile prefectorial authority went to younger and less experienced boys ; and the whole school, especially in the upper part, was naturally unsettled by the prospect of their future. Concentration on work became difficult. Discipline suffered. The Prefects' Minute Book during the war years (and indeed until about 1920) is concerned less with the usual peccadilloes of ragging and smoking than with bullying, general indiscipline, and an unhealthy moral atmosphere. Later in the war the food shortage began to make itself felt. Editorials in the *Malvernian* in 1918 put a cheerful face on things : 'We do not seem to be suffering greatly. The corpulent are still corpulent, and the slender are not yet skinny', the Editor says in March ; and in June : 'In spite of the oppression of Ration Tickets, we are yet living on the fat of the land' ; but the fat of the land consisted of potatoes mixed with margarine. One O.M. remembers 'the rush to the Grub on the infrequent arrival of a meagre chocolate assignment', and Preston recalls that 'the cheek-bones of the adolescent boy were unpleasantly prominent'.

As at the time of the Boer War, the *Malvernian* again printed letters from O.M.s at the front. They mostly dealt with military matters as far as the censorship would allow ; but one of those letters took issue with a master who had asked in an earlier number whether there was really any point in playing Rugby football for only half a term — had it not much better be given up altogether ? 'Rugger must stay,' wrote the O.M. 'What a confession of weakness to give it up now !' The letter is datelined, 'The Somme, 14th Nov. 1916'.

The reports on the Debating Society during the war years show that boys were much concerned with the moral issues the war presented. Is a nation entitled to advance its own interests at the expense of every other nation? Are reprisals justifiable? Can submarine warfare be defended? On all these matters the divisions were very close; and it is perhaps not a coincidence that when a master, H. B. Davies, started a Discussion Society in 1917 he should read the first paper on the subject of 'International Morality'. There was also a debate on whether there should be compulsory war work during the vacation. The tone of the debate was light-hearted and the motion was lost by an 'overwhelming majority'. Perhaps the boys felt that with two corps parades a week, with turning out ammunition in the Engineering Shop under the guidance of Kempson, and with the Malvern Y.M.C.A. Hut near St Omer to which they and the O.M. Society between them had contributed £1,000, they should at least be free from compulsory war work during the holidays. Their country would make a serious enough call on them soon enough.

Altogether 2,833 Malvernians are known to have served in the First World War. Of these 457 were killed and 1,100 were mentioned in despatches or otherwise honoured. When the war had ended, a Memorial Fund was started and the fallen were commemorated with three memorials. Alfred Drury, the Royal Academician, designed the noble statue of St. George in the Quadrangle. It forms the centre of the annual Remembrance Service. As the bugle sounds from the College tower, St. George looks out over the bowed heads of the boys on the Terrace, over the valley, into the infinite skies beyond. Few statues can express so perfectly the idea of young manhood gone to its last rest. It is simply inscribed 'To Our Brothers'. The names themselves are written on oak panels on the north side of the Chapel Chancel. The statue and the panels were unveiled in 1922. Three years later the Memorial Library, designed by Maurice Webb, was opened. It houses books of interest to non-specialists. The building also has a room set aside for the use of Old Malvernians, and another one which is the office of the Secretary of the O.M. Society. The third room was intended to be a kind of club-room for Sixth Formers ; * but they remained so attached to the studies in their houses and made so little use of it that eventually it became another class-room.

Armistice Day of 1918 found most of the boys, their resistance undermined by a long spell of rationing, stricken down by Spanish influenza. An O.M., D. R. Nieper, recalls that he was down at the Sanatorium and had already sufficiently recovered to be allowed in the reading-room downstairs. Maroons going off on the railway lines were the expected indication that the Armistice had been signed. When they went off, Nieper strummed out the National Anthem on the piano. Upstairs, the feverish but excited boys stood on their beds in their pyjamas and sang the anthem to the piano below.

In the following term, the Editorial of the *Malvernian* wrote, 'The influenza germ was able to produce greater changes here in a week than the Kaiser and his forces in four whole years'. The horse-drawn 'Pest-Wagon' [1] which always transported boys to the Sanatorium, worked overtime. Preston carries on the story :

'One day only 25 boys attended for School and Chapel, and eleven masters were still standing to teach them. Possibly will-power helped the survivors. The Army Entrance Examination was on at the time and one Woolwich candidate, a future distinguished general, when walking down College Road was greeted by the enquiry, "How are things going, Wansbrough-Jones ?" "Very full of brandy, Sir" was the retort. The awkward crisis was when I was summoned by his wife to the Medical Officer's bedside one morning early to find him delirious and really ill. No local doctor was prepared to spare me any time at all, so in this predicament, with only four trained nurses besides House Matrons and one or two V.A.D.s, I telegraphed to Colonel Earle at the War

* O.M.s in Ceylon collected money for the furniture that went into it.

Office,* to tell him of the position ; and within two hours had the reply, "Capt. West, R.A.M.C., from Leeds, seconded to your contingent to join this evening". He arrived about nine o'clock, and I accompanied him with a hurricane lamp while he made a tour of every house and the Sanatorium in the black-out. This he finished soon after midnight, and early the next morning organized the work throughout the School, concentrating the pneumonias, where movable, in the Sanatorium. As it was a fortnight before the M.O. could resume work, we had every reason to be grateful to his substitute, who worked quietly and cheerfully.'

One boy, C. V. Anderson, died during the epidemic ; and so did two masters : J. S. Keel and the much-loved H. W. Smith. Smith had been in failing health for some time. Hour after hour, in his room in South Lodge, whose walls were literally papered with photographs of his old pupils, he had worked through the long casualty lists to find the names of Malvernians, a task to break the heart of any devoted schoolmaster. Preston said of him in Chapel, 'Only a few knew that as recently as August the doctors had warned him how precarious was his health. On learning this, I wrote to offer to relieve the burden of his work. The answer was characteristic of the man : "I don't believe my work will do me any harm : I think indeed I should be just as miserable without it. . . . It is my deliberate choice to drop nothing. I doubt any serious risk : anyhow, I have a right to do as I please, and as, I think, duty bids." ' Besides the panelling in his class-room already referred to, his friends and pupils subscribed to endow the Memorial Exhibition in his name. It is held by boys in the form he used to teach.

There was one other crisis during these years which was, however, quite unconnected with the war and its aftermath. In 1918 the Chairman of the Council, Lord Beauchamp, found himself in disagreement with the other Council members on a personal matter unconnected with College affairs, and he re-

* He was the Council member nominated by the Army Council.

signed. Two months later, his solicitor wrote that Lord Beauchamp wanted to dissociate himself entirely from the School and therefore wished to sell School House.* The Council offered to buy it for £12,000 ; but the Earl asked for over twice that sum and this the Council was unable to pay. When a representative from Whitehall arrived, at Lord Beauchamp's request, to inspect the building as a possible home for paraplegics, it looked as if School House might really be lost to the College. The Monastery, further down College Road, happened to be up for sale at the time ; †️ and to make sure of at least some alternative accommodation, the Council bought that property for £4,500. In 1919, in fact, Lord Beauchamp issued a writ for the possession of School House, which the Council contested ; and in 1920 the Earl offered to sell the house to the College at a price to be fixed by arbitration, each side to bear its own legal costs so far incurred. To this the College agreed, and the arbitrator fixed the price at £13,500, a sum which was paid by the O.M. Society.

In this way there ended for a time the connection which had existed for over half a century between the College and Madresfield and to which, despite the unpleasantness at the end, the College had owed a very great deal. Today Malvern is glad to have the eighth Earl Beauchamp again as a member

---

* He was in fact selling a great deal of his property at that time. See *Berrow's Worcester Journal*, December 28, 1918, and February 8, 1919.

†️ This house has an interesting history. Built in 1851, it was from 1858 to 1886 the hydropathic establishment run by Dr. R. B. Grindrod, who soon rivalled Drs. Wilson and Gully in reputation. It was at that time known as 'Townsend House'. In 1891 the English Benedictine monks at Douai in France wanted an English centre for their work here. Townsend House, renamed 'Connellan College', was bought for that purpose, and the adjoining church was built in 1905. In 1903 the monks of Douai returned to England and settled at Woolhampton in Berkshire, but at first did not have enough accommodation there to dispense with the house in Malvern. By 1918, however, Douai Abbey at Woolhampton was big enough ; so the Monastery was sold to Malvern College. When the crisis about School House was over, the Monastery became the Music School ; and the monks' cells were ideally suited to become practice cubicles. (I owe the information in this footnote to the researches most generously undertaken by Dom Gregory Freeman, O.S.B., of Douai Abbey.)

of the Council. The successor of the seventh Earl as Chairman was Sir Paul Lawrence, a Judge of the High Court, an Old Malvernian *, and a brother of the three Lawrence sisters who founded Roedean School.†

By the time Sir Paul took office, the fall in numbers, which had begun in 1910 and had been much accelerated in the first year of the war, had been brought to a halt. In 1916 they began to rise again ; in 1918 they exceeded the previous record ; and in the summer of 1920 they reached exactly 574, this being the number of college shares which, it will be remembered, carried the right to a nomination. In 1923 the school was so full that Preston had to open a waiting house at 1, College Grove. Most other public schools were benefiting from a boom at about this time ; for the war had transferred a good deal of money into new hands, and the rising fees could be paid by many fathers who had not themselves been to public schools. The fees at Malvern rose from £105 in 1917 to £156 in 1921. Steep though this increase was, it was not unreasonable in view of the inflationary character of the period and of the extra commitments which the school now had to undertake. Preston was appalled at the salary list he found at Malvern, where the maximum that could be earned by a master who did not have a house was £300 p.a. ; and even after successive increases Malvern was never able to afford salaries which Preston considered sufficient to attract the best qualified men. In 1917 a Pension Scheme was introduced and the school set aside £1,000 a year for that purpose. Coupled with this was the introduction of the rule by which in normal circumstances a man would be asked to retire at the age of sixty. In 1923 the three housemasters who had held their houses since before the fifteen-year tenure had been introduced for new appointments were invited to relinquish them when

* He was a founder-member of the Old Malvernian Masonic Lodge, which was consecrated in 1922 with Norman Morice as first Master.

† He was also Chairman of the Council of Roedean. For the very full part he played in the history of his sisters' school, see *Roedean School, 1885 to 1955*, by Dorothy E. de Zouche.

they had completed thirty years in their house. When Toppin and Lyon did so in 1926, an era seemed to have come to an end.

Salary increases and pensions were not the only new charges on the finances of the school ; for it was also acquiring new property at this time. The purchase of the Monastery in 1919 has already been referred to. In 1920 Nos. 3 and 4 The Lees were bought and the Science facilities were expanded. Hitherto all science teaching had taken place in a few rooms behind the Pavilion. Preston was always anxious to increase the accommodation for science and he was backed up by strong recommendations from His Majesty's Inspectors. Finances were too tight to allow of anything very grandiose at that time, but the large stables of Radnor House were converted into something quite respectable and they are still in use today as the Geography Block. The building of a house for the Bursar in 1925 completes the list of operations undertaken by the College, though, as we shall presently see, the Old Malvernian Society made several very important additions to the school property during those same years.

The financial activities of the O.M. Society were in fact of immense importance. Almost all the share capital had by now been acquired by the Society — the last share was bought in 1928 — and in 1918 it embarked on its long task of buying up the debentures of the school.

In 1919 the scattered debenture debt was consolidated : all the old debentures were exchanged for new ones paying five per cent interest and secured on the whole property of the College. The architect of this scheme was the Society's Secretary, Henry Kempson. Kempson had been a boy at Malvern and in 1892 had come back to teach there. He remained on the staff until 1926 ; but his true vocation lay less in the class-room than in organizing the various schemes of the Society whose Secretary and Treasurer he had been since the very beginning in 1895. On committees which were composed mainly of experienced and prominent businessmen, it was the schoolmaster whose fertile mind initiated much of the work, who had a genius with figures and had an overall view which enabled him to think ahead in terms of years and not simply in terms of the annual balance sheet. In large matters a visionary, in small matters meticulous to a degree, he was well described by Preston as 'a craftsman in his every instinct', with an ill-concealed impatience for what he considered poor work that sometimes made him a difficult man to deal with. Malvern owes him a very great deal, of which the memorial brass in the Chapel is a small token.

When the consolidation had been carried through, the College still found itself with a debt of about £121,000. The school set aside £2,000 a year for debt redemption ; from 1932 onwards this obligation was taken over by the Society, which continued to buy up debentures whenever possible. The great advantage for the College was that more and more the interest on the debentures was paid to the Society instead of to outsiders, and the Society of course used the income it derived from the school for the latter's benefit. This interest became a considerable part of the Society's income, though it had other sources too. Until 1928 it received from the College the nomination fees on a certain number of the shares held by the Society. There were the profits from the school shop and store ; and legacies were generally made to the Society and not to the school direct, in order to avoid unnecessarily increasing the value of the property on which the debentures were secured. Finally, the Society had an income from the subscriptions of Old Malvernians. In 1925 much of that money was paid into the new O.M. Club, which was formed in order to keep separate for tax purposes the work done by the Society (now called simply the Malvernian Society) for the school and that done for its Old Boys.

Obviously a situation in which the school was financially so dependent on the Society for any extraordinary expenditure could have been a very tricky one ; but Preston writes that on no single occasion did any friction arise between the Society as such and the headmaster. Henry Kempson and later his successors, H. G. C. Salmon, R. B. Porch, and C. B. Lace all regarded it as axiomatic that under no circumstances should the Society attempt to control the policy of the Council. All four men were on the teaching staff and so were in a very strong position to know exactly what the real needs of the school were. With other prominent members of the Society this could not necessarily be taken for granted ; and it was for that reason that in 1925 S. P. Richardson, the Chairman of the Society, was appointed to the Council's Finance Committee.

However, there can be no question that even before that time, Council and Society were fully agreed on the desirability of the property that was bought by the latter during those years. An additional football field, the central plot of the Lees Estate, and 1, College Grove were bought in 1923. In 1924 the owners of the Firs Estate, which comprised thirty-six acres immediately south of the College grounds, were contemplating selling the land to a speculative builder — a step which would have brought the town all round the school. Preston, who later became a most active member of the Hills Conservation Board, intensely disliked urbanization. The Society agreed with him, stepped in, and bought the Estate. In 1927 the new School Shop was opened. Perhaps the most elegant building in the grounds, it was designed by an O.M., Howard Robertson, a later President of the Royal Institute of British Architects. The work on it had been a little slow, and one can sense from the editorials of the *Malvernian* how impatient the boys were to eat their buns in roomier surroundings. Six hard tennis courts were laid down in the Firs in 1927 and two more in 1933 ; and two squash courts were built in 1933 out of a bequest made by a relative to S. P. Richardson personally. The Society also bore the cost of having the School Crest officially approved and registered with the College of Heralds as a Coat of Arms.

But the greatest benefaction by the Society during this period was what it did in connection with the Royal Charter.

As early as 1879 the Council had hoped for the grant of such a charter ; but in the then financial state of the College, this was really out of the question. The conditions under which a charter is granted are that the institution in question ceases to be run for the profit of private individuals and that it is financially sound. The advantage, apart from the important aspect of prestige, is that the school is not taxed as a trading concern. To fulfil the two conditions, all the shares had to be surrendered to the new Corporation — it was for this purpose that the Society then bought the few shares it did not yet own — and it was felt that an extra effort would have to be made to reduce the debenture debt. In 1928, therefore, the Society issued an appeal for the surrender of debentures and set an example by giving up £9,100 of those it held at the time. Mr C. W. Dyson Perrins made the truly princely gift of £8,650 of debentures.* Altogether the appeal brought in some £20,800, and the debt was reduced to £95,000. The Royal Charter was granted by the Privy Council in 1929, and henceforth the word 'Ltd.' disappeared from the official name of Malvern College. R. B. Porch writes, 'It marked the completion of the most important of the tasks foreseen by those who founded the Society in 1895, the most important task, perhaps, that it will ever be called upon to undertake'.[2] This reflection must have given great satisfaction to Kempson when, having seen this work through, he retired later that year.

Hopes that the Royal Charter would usher in a period of steady, if gradual, financial improvement were destroyed by the Great Depression, the main impact of which struck England in 1931. Writing of its effects on the public schools, Preston says, 'It was not only that with the call for national and individual economy one's castles in the air were shattered and hopes indefinitely postponed ; but in the new situation in every home education became before everything else a ques-

---

* Three years later he also gave 'Ashfield' to the school. It was originally intended to be a house for the headmaster.

tion of finance.   In some cases incomes had for a time disappeared, in others uncertainty called for a revision of planning
and a reluctance to undertake fresh commitments.   The cost
of eight or nine years of a boarding school education had
never been small, and there was also the expense of after-
school training to be met.   Even parents who formerly
assumed that for reasons of tradition, fashion, or social prestige
their sons would go to the Public School of their choice, found
themselves calculating what degree of sacrifice was justified.
Surely there might be obtainable "something off the peg"
that would be an adequate substitute for the suit from an
expensive tailor.'

Numbers fell heavily, from 577 at the beginning of the
school year in 1930 to 465 three years later.   The most stringent
economies were necessary.   In 1931 a committee reporting on
possible economies in the school produced a report of twenty-
two pages.   Masters agreed unanimously to a five per cent cut
in their salaries — cuts which were not fully restored until a
new salary scale was introduced after the war — in order to
provide a fund to enable boys who would otherwise have
had to leave to remain at school, and the careers of over forty
boys were thus saved.   Housemasters had additional worries,
for it will be remembered that at that time they still ran the
houses on their own account ; and there was much anxious
correspondence with prep. school headmasters.   At the Speech
Days of 1932, 1933, and 1934 Preston begged parents if they
could possibly help it not to withdraw their boys early, and
urged how harmful it would be for the boys themselves.   It
did not even follow that a boy who left early would easily
find employment ; and though the Malvern Appointments
Committee, which had been started in 1920 by Nevil Smart
(O.M.), did its best, it could not place every boy who asked
for help.*   As for the effects on the school of early leaving,

---

* In 1934 the Headmasters' Conference set up a Public Schools Appointments Board ; but the College preferred to work in a more personal way
through its own committee.

Preston pointed out how the prefect system would suffer if there were not a sufficient number of boys with a sense of responsibility and of the age to control others. He showed that the average age in School House had fallen from 16·1 in September 1931 to 15·6 in September 1933, with only seven boys remaining beyond the age of seventeen. In No. 7 there was not a single boy over sixteen, not even the Head of House. That school cricket and football sides were young and in-experienced was another by-product of the situation, which much distressed the *laudatores temporis acti*, both on its own account and also because some of them thought that at a time of falling numbers, Malvern should try its utmost to attract more boys by making the most of its athletic reputation.

It was indeed a bitter blow to the school that, just as its financial position was improving, the Depression should have held back its economic progress. It was at any rate some consolation that it seemed to affect progress in other fields hardly at all.

In particular, there was during Preston's headmastership a broadening of interest in things of the mind. This did not mean that there was an increase in the number of university scholarships, for the teaching of the best boys had always been excellent. The successes in this field had been, if anything, somewhat greater before the war than after it, partly, perhaps, because public schoolboys were beginning to compete for awards with boys from grammar schools at about this time. There was a rather lean patch between 1926 and 1934, though in 1937 eight awards were won. But university scholarships, important though they are as a guide to a school's academic distinction, are not necessarily a reliable indication of the intellectual life of those who are not groomed for scholarships, or indeed of the breadth of education in the Sixth Form. In these respects Preston found much that he wanted to change when he first came to Malvern.

'The curriculum in vogue at Malvern in 1914', he writes, 'appeared to me hardly to correspond with the ideas being worked out elsewhere in what was the dawn of the age of transition. It was conventional and adequate only by Victorian standards, and even then narrow and uninspiring. There was a Classical Side of four forms, in the bottom of which most, if not all, Scholars and Exhibitioners started. The numbers in these forms were small, thus ensuring careful and individual teaching. . . . The result of this good teaching had shown itself in the University Scholarship record. I inherited a Classical Sixth containing four excellent scholars, and it is interesting to note that these four, all of the same year, have since occupied the positions of Permanent Secretary to the Colonial Office,* Clerk to the London County Council,† High Commissioner in Canada, ‡ and Editor of *The Listener*.§ There was only one boy reading advanced History under a part-time specialist, and one working for a scholarship in Mathematics (which he obtained eventually). . . . The top set in science consisted chiefly of would-be medicos and practically no University candidates. On the Modern side there was a Modern Fifth which the form master was allowed by his own choice to enter for the School Certificate, but apart from the Classical Sixth taking the Higher Certificate of the Oxford and Cambridge Board, the only outside examination candidates were a few in a large form called the Matriculation Form who aimed at the London Matriculation. Those who were to go to Oxford and Cambridge and had not the brains to pass "smalls" or "little-go" unaided, were collected in another group, whose form master was alleged, not without some truth, to read aloud the crib for the set books at either university alternately. The roll of the Upper School was completed by the Army Class top set, under expert instruction and able to secure good places on the Woolwich list. Here were found most of the entrance scholars who did not take Classics.

'The general impression given was that Malvern in its

---

* Sir Charles Jeffries.   † Sir Eric Salmon.
‡ Sir Alexander Clutterbuck.   § A. E. W. Thomas.

Upper School provided an educational system that made it possible for boys to pass the necessary preliminary examinations for the services and the professions and also for admission to the Universities at the low standard demanded in 1914, and for gifted boys to obtain scholarships in Classics, and occasionally in Mathematics — in other words, gave parents the facilities of a good coaching establishment. This instruction was in the hands of well qualified teachers, most of them the older members of the Staff. There was little trace of any interchange of thought between either the teachers or the taught in the different departments, and any "out of school hours" activity in things "intellectual" appeared non-existent. There were a few lectures with magic lantern slides, but these were regarded as "Entertainments" and were treated as such ! The complete isolation of the houses in the evenings only added to this general impression that things of the mind ceased to have much importance once the key had been turned in the class-room door. This being so, it was not surprising that in the Middle and Lower Schools one found little that seemed purposeful or inspired. The Staff here consisted of men with the experience to exact a quota of industry and maintain (with the occasional exception) excellent discipline. They maintained a cheerful and not unwilling spirit among their pupils ; but it was plain that the qualifying standard for entry had been low and the number of sub-average entrants fairly large. . . . It only emphasized the general atmosphere of "industry and indifference" that future Army candidates were even at this stage kept apart in the Army Side "for fear that they should not realize the importance of starting early on a purposeful educational course". (Quotation.) . . .

'Faced with this comparative lack of intellectual interest, and knowing what was being said in every Common Room in England, if not possibly widely in the homes of the country, about over-athleticism at Malvern, I was naturally anxious to make sure which was the cause of the other and which the effect. Looking back now on those days, it should be pointed out to the censorious critic that the environment of a Malvern boy in 1914 was very different from what it is today. . . . The young saw far less of the world outside than modern transport enables them to do today. At Malvern, only members of the "archaeological society" (a euphemistic phrase !) and the Shooting Eight brought bicycles to school. There was no wireless, let alone television, and magazines with far less illustration provided the news of the world. There were no gramophones, and "musical appreciation" was only hardly acquired. It was the day of suffragettes and chaperones, and friendly free intercourse of boys and girls in adolescence was frowned upon, and in term time unthinkable. Malvern had no school tennis courts, and golf was only slowly being considered as a term time possibility. The public schoolboy was not as yet educated up to a wide liberty of movement, and "bounds" were strictly drawn in any urban district. Few schools (and Malvern was no exception) had the ground space for all to play games on half holidays. The alternative offered was yard games on asphalt or to run on a road to the White House (now replaced by a redbrick erection).* Music, Art, and Carpentry were all "extras" paid for by parents, only if their sons were gifted in such "side shows". There was no spacious general library available for the whole school in leisure hours, and the House Libraries mostly contained out-of-date (and out-of-repair) fiction. The reaction of an average or unintellectual boy to such an environment was pardonably that of either boredom or even discontent, and an atmosphere of enforced discipline only intensified this. As an escapist, where should he turn except to the more exciting field of sport, even if no "performer" himself ? There was little chance of peaceful reading as one of three or four in a study nine foot by six. . . .

'If the charge of over-athleticism was true, what should a Headmaster do ? . . . The only hope was surely if possible

---

* The spot is at the cross-roads just south of the site of the Three Counties Show.

to restore the balance and to discourage the disease in its worst manifestations. . . . It was, I felt, only possible to wean the average boy from regarding almost with idolatry those who possessed a natural flair for games and treating as V.I.P. the school colours of the past, if one could arouse his interest in other directions and widen his horizon. It was for this reason that, as soon as the end of the War made it possible, I set myself both by direct and indirect means to provide facilities for cultural needs as well as alternative occupations. A Memorial Reading Room and new tennis courts could equally serve my purpose, and it was from this point of view that I valued alike a Dramatic Society and a biological laboratory. . . .

'The School had a glimpse of my mind when I ruled that in future the Sixth should share with School Prefects the privilege of entering the School buildings by the central steps. This was a symbol the dullest mind could understand.' *

Symbolical was followed by practical action. In 1920 Preston invited the Board of Education to inspect the School for the first time. An inspection can be a great help to a head-master who wishes to make changes ; and on their next visit eleven years later, the inspectors referred to the 'undoubted intellectual improvement in the College' since the last occasion. The Higher and School Certificates were introduced ; and there was a shift away from putting most of the academic eggs into the classical basket. In particular, there was a great extension of the facilities for teaching Science. We have already seen how the stables of Radnor House were converted in 1920, and the Inspectors in 1924 thought that the new accommodation would serve its purpose for twenty years if necessary. Before half that time had elapsed, it became clear that the

---

* Understand, perhaps ; but not immediately appreciate ! A letter in the *Malvernian* of December 1915 signed 'An Inferior' says, 'May I take this opportunity of voicing the regret which I know is felt by the majority of the School at the loss of one of the oldest of our traditions ? Last Easter term the Sixth Form were allowed to make use of the steps and entrances to the College buildings, hitherto reserved for School Prefects alone. Malvern has, as we are well enough aware, few traditional customs ; is it not a pity to sweep away the only ones we have ?' Boys can be very conservative.

demands for scientific education were expanding a good deal faster than the Inspectors had anticipated ; but when Preston raised the matter in 1934 the Council thought that, if a new Science School were to be built at this time of general economy, the money could only be raised by an appeal. To this appeal there was a generous response, notably a gift of a covenant for £1,000 annually for seven years from Arthur Manners. The whole cost of £21,000 was eventually raised by O.M.s and friends of the College. The Science Schools were named after Preston and opened in 1938 by Earl Baldwin. When the architect, P. W. Hubbard (O.M.), first submitted his plans in 1935, a member of the Council questioned 'the somewhat ample nature of the accommodation provided in the scheme', but was satisfied when Preston explained that 'provision was being made also for the future — say thirty years'. Events were to overtake his estimate as they had overtaken that of 1924.

The introduction of Spanish, Specialist Biology, and for a time of a 'Business Fifth' completes the account of modernizations in the actual teaching ; and Preston could point to the success of this widening of the curriculum when the fourteen Firsts won by O.M.s at Oxford and Cambridge in 1929 and 1930 were taken from seven different faculties. But the changes outside the class-room were equally important.

Pride of place probably belongs to the developments in school music. Here the acquisition of the Monastery in 1919 made possible the provision of more satisfactory practice rooms than the accommodation in 4, The Lees ; * and when Lyon had left for war service, his place as musical director had been taken by F. H. Shera, who had been recommended to Preston by Sir George Dyson, formerly a colleague of Preston's at Marlborough. Shera was a man of enormous energy and a genius at inculcating musical appreciation. The

---

* That house has more distinguished musical associations : it was Elgar's home for a few months in 1889. (Smith, *op. cit.* Chapter XII ; Diana M. McVeagh, *Edward Elgar*, p. 15.)

music notice-board sprouted notices about practices for a Choral Society, an Ensemble Class, and a Harmony Class ; and within a year the school orchestra was able to put on a concert which included Grieg's Holberg Suite, Wagner's Siegfried Idyll, two short pieces for strings by Elgar and Percy Grainger, and Mozart's great G minor Symphony (March 1917). The programmes were not always as ambitious as this, nor were all the concerts given by boys ; but between March 1917 and February 1923 there were no fewer than 100 concerts, or about five concerts a term — this exclusive of the fortnightly organ recital given by Shera in the Chapel. From 1922 to 1926 the boys, under Shera's guidance, also brought out a magazine called *The Concert-Goer*, which appeared five times a term and included programme notes for the forthcoming concerts. In 1928 Shera left to become Professor of Music at Sheffield University (of which Sir William Hadow, O.M., himself a great musicologist, was then Vice-Chancellor) and was succeeded by J. A. Davison, who carried on the good work. The whole school took part in performances of oratorios, with every boy joining in singing some of the chorales. One such performance, of Bach's Christmas Oratorio, was broadcast in 1930.

Besides music, there was an enormous proliferation of societies to carry on out-of-school activities. True, that stalwart of the past, the Debating Society, died out almost completely after approving of the Russian Revolution in November 1917 ; and the substitute of a School Parliament, complete with Cabinet and Opposition Front Bench lived barely two years. Only when there was a General Election outside, in 1929 and 1931, did debating revive for the occasion. All this may be partly due to Preston's nervousness about masters expressing their views on political or religious issues in the class-room : 'It was really in those days more a point of etiquette than of principle', he writes. 'To discuss politics in school or with boys except in a purely objective form was something "not done". This was the tradition inherited from earlier days, when boys in public schools found amusement in the knowledge that Common Room was divided in politics. The young remained Tory "on principle", and it was not till the Varsity that some of them blossomed out as Radicals for a season. A socialist master was little more than an encouragement to the "intellectual" Sixth former to prove him wrong.'

It could also be argued that, useful as it is for a boy to learn to present a case in public, debates, with their encouragement to the speaker to express only one side of the question and to use debating tricks, are in themselves a poor form of intellectual exercise. One will get nearer the truth in discussion than in debate ; and in this boys at Malvern had some training. In 1917 a Discussion Society was formed ; it met fortnightly, sometimes more frequently ; a boy, or occasionally a master (the Masters' Common Room had a discussion society of its own), would read a paper which the rest would then discuss for the rest of the evening. In March 1920, the Discussion Society began to produce a literary magazine called *The Beacon*, with John Wheeler-Bennett as its first editor. It appeared more or less regularly until 1936 and showed a standard of writing worthy of the handsome quality paper on which it was printed.

Gradually all this began to have an effect on other parts of the school. In 1918 School House revived *The Magpie*, which had previously been published from 1891 to 1896 ; and, above all, the *Malvernian* itself became a much more interesting and rather more mature publication. In 1932 the editorials, which had once been mere catalogues of the term's weather, games, and principal events, all of which were recorded in other parts of the magazine, began to take on the appearance of leading articles, a little sententious at times, but with some claim to thought and style.

Regular drama also had its beginning at this time. After 1918 there were some house plays and other occasional performances, all of which prepared the ground for School Plays which began in 1929, cautiously at first, with small casts and the women's parts played by women. But by 1932 the name part in Shaw's *Saint Joan* was played by a boy. For some years the School Play took place at Speech weekend in the summer term. In the Christmas term, it was the turn of the masters to appear on the stage for the entertainment of the school. The first occasion was in 1929. After 1932 the Masters' Play was moved to Shrove Tuesday. Ever since 1890 there had been a Concert on Shrove Tuesday, usually given by visiting artistes. It became an increasingly light-hearted affair, and in 1919 it was no longer called a Concert but an Entertainment. After that its character continued to change. The programmes became less musical and more dramatic. Outside performers appeared less frequently and boys more often ; but the boys have found the spectacle of their masters appearing in un-accustomed rôles so piquant that their play became a permanent fixture.

Other Societies which flourished during this time were a Play-Reading Society, a Wireless Society, a Railway Society, a Photographic Society, and a Mathematical Discussion Society. There was also *La Société Française*, which in 1937 gave a per-formance to the school of *Le Médecin Malgré Lui* ; the Laletes Club, which was a Discussion Society for the Fifth Form ; and the English Club. This last was formed in 1932 'with the sole aim of promoting self-entertainment'; and in one term (Christmas 1932) it produced two debates, a play-reading session, an Eisteddfod evening, a mock session of the League of Nations, and an evening of Modern Verse Grave and Gay. It owed a good deal of inspiration to R. Allison, and when he left in 1936 (he later became headmaster of Brentwood), it became known as the Allison Club. At that time it had a membership of 250 boys.

Of course not all the societies were as well attended as this ; and some of them held their meetings more sporadically than others ; but this record leaves no doubt that Preston's aim of widening the boys' interests was being achieved. On

Speech Day of 1933 Preston said, 'I believe in these days it is even more important to educate for leisure than to educate for salesmanship. I believe that a person who knows how to use his spare time never wastes any time.' And elsewhere he writes, 'Some of my aims were slowly being realized. It was not perhaps anything very marked or revolutionary, but I was conscious that the attitude of the ordinary boy to his work was improving without outside pressure, the gulf between the athlete and the intellectual was narrowing, and the "average boy" seemed less inclined in his "middle age" to be disgruntled or to mark time until he was called upon to make a "last year's effort". I fancy the climate in the preparatory schools was also changing, and new boys arrived less prepared to regard themselves as people of no importance, and often with interests that they were anxious to develop.' It is also interesting to note that of the six university award winners in 1932/3, five were heads of their houses and only one of these was a good games player. Since no housemaster or headmaster would want to appoint as heads of houses boys who did not have considerable standing in the eyes of the school, this suggests that boys were now ready to follow the lead of seniors who were not necessarily distinguished on the games field.

Fagging of course was scarcely modified. Fags still sat in their studies with one foot out in the corridor so as to have a good start when there was a fag-call. They still made toast for the prefects by holding slices of bread before the gas-fire with their bare hands because the toast was not allowed to show the marks of a toasting fork. 'The provision of toasting forks was mooted from time to time,' writes an O.M., 'but was invariably turned down by the fags themselves as being effeminate and less capable of producing the true toast-maker's chef d'œuvre.'

Excessively arbitrary prefectorial power had been curtailed quite early in Preston's headmastership. An O.M. records that in his time (1916 to 1921) the use of caning as a punishment underwent a big change. 'When I arrived there, one could be caned for the slightest incident, including being the last to arrive in response to the call for "Fag" or "Boy"; and, what is more, with anything from a slipper or a Rackets handle to a steel-centred riding crop. . . . When my turn came to administer corporal punishment, details had to be recorded in a punishment book, and a regulation cane produced by the master authorizing its use.'

Ten years later things seem to have slipped back a bit, at least in some houses. One O.M. describes the 'cat-and-mouse' atmosphere which the prefects in his house created for the fags. Another writes that in his house, prefects found 'unwritten house rules' a useful pretext for beatings. 'My greatest moment of triumph was when I refused to be beaten for such an imaginary "offence" and actually succeeded in persuading the Head of House to abolish all "unwritten" House rules. Unfortunately, the Housemaster soon found out, and the reign of terror returned, if possible, more ruthless than before.' *

A contemporary of his sends this description of what happened to a culprit who had offended : 'Retribution, if it followed, usually followed quickly, but never till after house prayers, that is to say, not until the victim was undressed and ready for bed, in his dormitory or cubicle. The Prefects would gather in the Pres' Room, and the junior of their number would be sent to summon the defaulter. The bedroom door would be flung open, or the cubicle curtain roughly pulled aside, and the messenger of the gods would demand, "Smith, you are wanted in the Pres' Room in pyjamas !" The messenger was gone. A wan smile to one's fellows, a hasty shuffle into slippers and dressing gown, and then, with heart in throat, down the flight of stone stairs . . . along the

---

* If this action by the Housemaster seems difficult to believe, it should be remembered that at that time some of the older men took a hierarchy for granted even in the Masters' Common Room and made a new arrival on the staff very conscious of his place on the lower rungs. Bullock, the genial Second Master, did much to change this state of affairs, and the Second World War did the rest.

by-now-darkened study passages to the shut door of the Pres'
Room ; a timid knock ; "Come in !" The Pres' Room
seemed a blaze of light, and ranged around its walls, on which
hung boards with the names of past prefects, were seated in
fairly easy chairs the eight or nine prefects of the house.
They seemed to be all knees and grey flannel trousers. The
table, covered with a dark, ink-stained cloth, normally in the
middle of the room, had been pushed to one end, and a chair
with a semi-circular back was drawn up close to and facing it.
The Head of House snapped out a few words of accusation
and demanded to know if the victim had anything to say ;
but by then it did not matter. "Take off your dressing-gown.
—Bend over." It was not enough just to bend over the back of
the chair. The head must be under the table and the backside
facing the ceiling. Then the running swing with the whippy
house-shoe, its body reinforced with an old table-knife and its
sole hardened with such things as the flat ends of drawing pins.
Perhaps there would be four or five or six strokes. Then, as
one craved most for sympathy or admiration or interest, or a
mixture of all three, the hardest cut of all, delivered in a tone
of utter contempt : "Get up. Get out." There was never
time to put on one's dressing-gown, but one might have been
beaten again if one had left it there.' The author concludes
his account, 'I bear not the slightest resentment against these
proceedings, nor did they make me unhappy at the time',
and, besides, he is able to say that by the time he left in 1932
there was a great deal less beating by prefects than there had
been when he arrived in 1927.

Not everyone came to so philosophical a conclusion. The
1920s and 1930s produced a spate of writers, mostly novelists,
who reflected caustically about the various public schools they
had attended. Malvern was fortunate in that, apart from an
essay written by Derek Verschoyle in a symposium of rather
sardonic reminiscences from former public school boys, the
one novel about it was written by a boy of fifteen and published
only abroad. 'Exposures' of the public school system had an

avid public in those days, and they led Preston to comment drily one Speech Day that happy is the school that has no novelist. At any rate in the 1930s life at Malvern seems to have been a good deal kinder than before to small boys and to those who were not particularly good at games.

Games continued to be played with distinction ; and Preston, who relates that as a Marlborough housemaster he had been criticized for being, if anything, too enthusiastic about games, was happy to see Malvern achievements continue. There were many great names in Malvern cricket in this period. N. E. Partridge was considered by Toppin the greatest all-round cricketer the school ever produced. An example of this was his amazing performance in the two-day match against Repton in 1918, when he scored 229 not out and took ten wickets for 150. He was invited to play for the Gentlemen while still at school and later played for Cambridge and for Warwickshire. G. B. Cuthbertson later played for Middlesex and captained Northamptonshire. C. G. W. Robson, a violent driver of the cricket ball, played for Middlesex ; J. A. Deed, a batsman of quiet elegance and style, for Kent, as did C. J. Capes. The Eleven of 1922 included six first-class players : the greatest of these, E. R. T. Holmes, was to captain Oxford and later Surrey, and played for England against the West Indies in 1934 and against South Africa in 1935. G. B. Legge, the captain of that 1922 Eleven, also captained Oxford, captained Kent, and played for England against South Africa in 1927 and against New Zealand in 1929. The other four county players of that year were S. T. Jagger, T. B. G. Welch, and two sons of Malvern masters, C. G. Toppin and J. W. Greenstock. Other first-class cricketers later in this period were W. H. Bradshaw, W. H. L. Lister, R. G. Stainton, A. H. Brodhurst, and R. H. Maudsley.

Toppin gave up his control over the cricket in 1924, after thirty-seven years. In his later years he rarely played in the nets himself and taught by precept rather than by example.

His successor, Charles Fiddian-Green, who was a most elegant and graceful batsman, played a good deal in the nets, so that during the next eleven years 'his methods were watched, imbibed, and copied' by many Malvern cricketers.[3] Both Toppin and Fiddian-Green had the help of 'Father' Tate, who had succeeded George Arber in 1904 as coach and for the next thirty-two years was indefatigable in the nets and the grounds. 'Curbed perhaps in some measure by the dominating C. T., and thus coaching to order, as it were, he yet gave many useful hints and advice to those to whom he bowled. And he bowled so accurately, too, and could serve up continuously a series of half-volleys — or other types of delivery — to order, when C. T. stood behind urging the young player that half-volleys were a gift straight from the gods, and must be hit and not gently patted.' [4]

In football also there were many triumphs to record during those years. In 1927 and 1928 all four school matches were won ; and the Old Malvernians won the Arthur Dunn Cup for three years in succession (1924, 1925, and 1926) and again in 1928. The Public Schools Rackets Cup was brought home three times during this period : by C. G. W. Robson and J. A. Deed in 1920, and by P. D. Manners and N. W. Beeson in 1936 and 1937. The Quadrangular Boxing Competition with Clifton, Cheltenham, and Downside began in 1926 with a win for Malvern ; but this achievement was not to be repeated until 1938. Another new event in the sporting calendar was the Athletics Match against Shrewsbury, which began in 1934. The standard of athletics was rising fast throughout the whole country and at every public school as it was being taken more seriously ; and the 1930s saw a considerable number of new Malvern records set up, some of which still stand today. But Preston disliked the cult of individual stardom which was being promoted by the Press ; and to discourage it at Malvern he even abolished in 1934 the cup that used to be awarded to the 'Champion Athlete'. This kind of stardom he felt was bad for the individual and

harmful to the team-spirit which he considered to be the most
important justification for games at school.

The Corps was in a less flourishing state than before the
war, when Capt. D. S. M. Tassell had had practically every boy
in the Corps. In the school and in the country at large there
was a reaction against military matters after the war, and
Tassell's successors, Major H. D. E. Elliott, Capt. F. Hare, and
Capt. H. M. Robinson found themselves hampered by the
indifference or hostility of parents to such things as the annual
camp, during the years when the Peace Ballot was making the
headlines. Preston himself had no sympathy with this view,
and on several speech days he urged parents to be more cooperative and reported to them the great importance which
the War Office attached to the O.T.C. as the best source of
officers for future contingencies.

At that time the Corps still held joint Field Days with
other public schools in the neighbourhood. The first of these
after the war was held at Chipping Sodbury in 1919. Of this
occasion Preston writes :

'During the "battle" one Malvern platoon became isolated
and set upon by a large contingent of Downside, who, possibly
ignorant of the regulations governing such encounters, charged
with "fixed bayonets"! In the struggle Sgt. Palfreman of No.
4 was run through the hand by a bayonet, but the timely
arrival of an umpire saved further bloodshed. After the "cease
fire" all the officers, both masters and boys, were summoned to
a "pow-wow" in a tent, while the rank and file took their tea
in marquees. When Downside emerged from tea, they found
their rifles had been re-piled upside down in the mud, but
Malvern were disappearing on their way to the station, having
been tactfully withdrawn by a School House Sergeant-Major
with some acumen on his own responsibility. In the upshot,
the Malvern C.O. took disciplinary action and made his peace
with his Downside colleague, who had had to "indent in
triplicate" for a number of missing bolts believed to be
adorning as trophies studies at Malvern. I should have had

H. C. A. GAUNT, HEADMASTER 1937 to 1953
(drawing by H. A. Freeth)

F. S. PRESTON, HEADMASTER 1914 to 1937
(drawing by H. A. Freeth)

no official cognizance of the affair had I not received a week later a letter from a friend in the War Office, saying that unofficially their lordships of the Army Council "wished to be reassured that there was no religious feeling behind the incident" ! My assurance was so successful that the War Office with no great tact brigaded Malvern and Downside together the next month at camp. I felt constrained on the last day of term to give a hint of my knowledge, when, in wishing the Corps a successful Camp, I hoped they would bring us credit by their conduct and not turn the camp "upside downside".'

One eminent survivor of that bayonet charge does indeed recall that Malvern's battle-cry on that occasion was 'To Hell with the Pope !' ; but that religious feeling was not really the cause of the incident might be deduced from the fact that at the Camp three years later Malvern became involved with a perfectly protestant school, Dulwich. An O.M. writes, 'On the last night the entire Malvern contingent were told that Dulwich School were going to attack us ; so we sat up all night armed, prepared, and ready with tent-hammers etc. In the morning we discovered that they had heard the same about us and had spent an equally sleepless night fruitlessly.'

All this shows perhaps that the Corps Camp evoked a suitably martial ardour among the boys. On a different type of camp Malvernians proved themselves a good deal more pacific. These were the years of the Duke of York's Camps. In 1921 the Duke, later King George VI, began to organize camps in which he brought together 200 public school boys and 200 working-class boys for a week every summer in an attempt to bridge the social gulf between them. Since only two boys went from any one school each year, it cannot be said that a large number of Malvernians were affected. Far more boys, however, went annually to the hop-picking camp which the School Mission began to organize for the people of Canning Town in 1923. In 1928 we read that fifty-four

Malvernians applied to go to the camp that year (though in the end only twelve could go). From 1923 onwards the school also sent two boys each term to spend a weekend in Canning Town ; and occasionally there were football matches, either in Malvern or in the East End, between a team from the College and one from the boys' clubs.

The work of the Mission was now under the charge of Kennedy-Cox. When the war was over, Tinley moved to another parish, and Kennedy-Cox offered to take over the work on condition that he was given control and a free hand. He would look for a certain proportion of maintenance from the school, but beyond that he would make himself responsible for raising funds elsewhere for the expansion that he envisaged. In the event Kennedy-Cox's work soon spread beyond Canning Town into neighbouring London Docks and then into Bristol and Southampton. The Dockland Settlement (as the Malvern Mission was renamed) became a vast national institution, and its architect's services were officially recognized with a knighthood in 1930. The school could guess at the dynamic character of Kennedy-Cox each term when he came to address them on Mission Sunday ; and especially in the years just after the war, record amounts were given during the collections — £64 were collected one Sunday in 1920. But these were of course only a drop in the bucket compared with the resources which Kennedy-Cox was able to raise outside the school ; and as the years passed and the Dockland Settlement grew, the feeling that Malvern had a particularly intimate connection with it almost inevitably began to weaken ; and Preston, while welcoming the enormous increase in the value of the social work done by the Settlement, was sorry that its educational value for the school should thereby be in some degree diminished.

Preston was always acutely aware that in a period when the public schools were meeting with much criticism, they could only justify themselves if they kept alive the spirit of service in their boys. On Speech Day in 1923 he pointed

out regretfully that government policy towards India had had
a discouraging effect on the kind of public school boy who
in earlier days would have gone to India in a spirit of service,
and that the operation of the Geddes Axe had similarly
reduced the number of boys who wanted to serve in the
Armed Forces. By 1926 the India Office was itself alarmed
at the falling off in recruitment to the Indian Army and the
Indian Civil Service from public schools ; and Preston commented on Speech Day that year that there was still great
scope for a life of service in the Empire.

But it was not only government policy which put the
young men off ; it was an increasingly materialistic spirit in
the middle classes as a whole. In 1929 Preston asked the
parents, 'Is there not a danger of the public school man
becoming a little too self-centred ? Who, for instance, is
undertaking the government of the country ? I do not mean
at Westminster so much as in the county, the district, and the
locality, because surely in the near future those who are going
to undertake that work are going to control Westminster
also. How far do public school men today undertake civic
and municipal work ? Or is it only their divine prerogative
to remain outside and indulge in an Englishman's privilege, a
healthy grumble ? That work has got to be undertaken by
people who are well informed. You do not become well
informed merely by sitting still in the class-room and being
well taught. The only well-informed men I know are men
who have read for themselves, thought for themselves, and
taught themselves. Therefore I believe that that portion of
the task is as much due (if not more) to the influence of the
home as it is to the influence of the School. So, in conclusion,
I am appealing to you that as you have sent your sons to a
public school, you will not expect the school, any more than
you would wish yourselves, to train them to regard the world
as a very pleasant playground in which their life's work was
to obtain a sufficient amount of this world's goods and to
have all its delights, but to bear and share responsibility side

by side with others with a wider vision and a self-trained mind.'*

It was perhaps in the 1920s that people realized that the world would never settle down again into the outlook of the pre-war era. The second half-century of Malvern's life would be shaped by this realization. The fiftieth anniversary of the College fell in 1915, during the war and was therefore not celebrated. Instead the ceremonies took place during the year of the Diamond Jubilee in 1925. Ten of the boys who had entered the school in its first term were still alive ; † and on January 25 the school sent to each of them the following telegram :

'Headmaster Masters and Boys of Malvern College send Greetings on her 60th birthday to the ten Survivors of her first term's entry.'

All ten of them replied. The answer of one of them, aged seventy-four, began, 'I came home from hunting on Saturday and found your "surprise" telegram'. Two others sent many pages of their reminiscences which were published in the *Malvernian* and provide a good deal of the material for the second chapter of this book.

In terms of the life of the school, the sixtieth anniversary marked more of a turning-point than the fiftieth would have done ; for the mid twenties saw the retirement of a large number of masters whose long years of service to the school had made them almost institutions. H. H. House gave up No. 4 after thirty years as a housemaster in 1923 and retired from the staff in 1929, having successfully trained nearly 130 classical scholars and exhibitioners in his time. He lived to a ripe old age, and at the age of ninety-three saw through the press a book of 'versions' of his own compositions in Latin and Greek. Charles Toppin retired from No. 6 in 1925 and

---

* Preston himself served as a County magistrate, as Chairman of the Juvenile Court, as Chairman of the Malvern Library Committee, as a Hills Conservator, and as a member of the Church Assembly.

† The last survivor, J. F. Cooksey, died twenty years later, at the age of ninety-five.

was due to retire from the staff in 1928. As the time for this drew near, he was increasingly unhappy, worried what would fill the place of the school in his life ; but he died in his last term. His daughter Mary later married J. S. Rambridge, and through them the Toppin encouragement of sportsmanship lived on and found a special home in No. 9, over which they were to preside for fifteen years after the war. Col. Lyon gave up No. 7 in 1925 and retired from the staff in 1927 after thirty-nine years. Others who left at about this time included C. T. Salisbury, the first housemaster of No. 8, after thirty-six years in the school ; and L. S. Milward (O.M.) after thirty-five years — he was born in the same year as the school and as people began to talk of the Centenary in 1965, Milward, who went on living in Malvern and frequently came to watch school matches, cherished the hope that he might live to see the Centenary. He died in 1961, at the age of ninety-six. D. J. P. Berridge, to whom Malvern Science owes so much and who had been Secretary of the Science Masters' Association from 1907 to 1910, gave up No. 1 in 1927 and left in the same year. He died in 1929 and in his will left the money to endow the Berridge Chemistry Prize.

The 1930s saw the death in 1933 of Henry Foster at the age of eighty-eight and, in the following year, of Canon James. W. W. Lowe (O.M.) left in 1932 after thirty-six years on the staff. He had been for many years in charge of Malvern football and had indeed been an exceptionally brilliant games player : a triple Cambridge Blue (cricket, football, and golf), a football international, a gold medallist at skating and skiing ; and his enthusiasm in these fields had had a great influence on his House (No. 8) and on the school at large. Col. Bullock also retired in 1932 after forty-three years. He had succeeded Toppin as Second Master ; and both men had had a term as acting headmaster — Toppin in 1915 when Preston was ill ; and Bullock in 1930, when the Headmaster was granted a sabbatical term by the Council. Unsparing in his work for the College, Bullock had also done much for the county, whose Deputy Lord-Lieutenant he was when he left Malvern.

A look at the Register will show the other changes on the Staff. Some of those who retired, like F. Brayne-Baker and R. T. C. Cookson, had come to Malvern in the last years of the nineteenth century. A word should also be said here about some of the College servants whose names are not recorded in the Register, but whom Old Malvernians will well remember — men like Laker, the inspiring Rackets professional from 1895 to 1925 and his equally dedicated successor Green ; Sgt. Windsor, who held the fort in the Grub every morning ; 'Sham' (E. Bruton), the College barber, whose farouche personality and ruthless work with the shears in his ill-lit shed next to the Swimming Bath is the subject of much comment in the correspondence columns of the *Malvernian* ; Sgt. Major 'Chow' Robinson of the O.T.C. ; 'Charlie' (F. Smith), who succeeded Prosser as School Porter — all these men retired in the second half of Preston's Headmastership. Another departure of a very different sort, but which somehow fits into the picture of the weakening links with the school as it was in the nineteenth century, is the disappearance of the ivy from the College walls in 1931.

In 1936 Preston felt that the time had come for him, too, to retire, and he did so at Easter in the following year. He was a powerful personality. Masters and boys alike remember him with a kind of awe. Personally, Preston was rather remote — he never addressed either a boy or a master by his Christian name — but everyone remembers him as a man of great wisdom. 'You might disagree with him quite strongly,' said one of his colleagues ; 'but deep down you always felt that he was right.' His rulings were not peremptory : he was always ready to consider sympathetically every reasonable suggestion, and his decisions were the result of careful thought. This did not make him a merely cerebral headmaster. Indeed, his greatness consisted in the ability to combine deep convictions with an open mind. He did not drift with every fashion of thought ; but neither was he excessively conservative. The school was fortunate that it had a headmaster who, though appointed before the First World War broke out, was able to guide Malvern into the directions called for by the post-war world.

CHAPTER VIII

The Headmastership of H. C. A. Gaunt
1937–1953

LIKE many of his predecessors, Gaunt was still in his thirties when he was appointed to succeed Preston. He had been educated at Tonbridge and was a scholar of King's College, Cambridge. He was a tennis and hockey Blue, and had played cricket for Warwickshire. He came to Malvern after having taught at King Edward's School, Birmingham, and at Rugby. He felt aware at once that the school, so far from having settled into a rut in the closing years of a long Headmastership, was looking to the future as much as to the past. On his first Speech Day he said, 'There is little of the spirit here that "what was good enough for our grandfathers will be good enough for our grandsons". I mean that the natural progress which has gone on during the last twenty years or more will be expected in years to come. This is one of the greatest legacies that a headmaster can bequeathe to his successor.' True, the more usual form of the tag he quoted refers to a span of two generations rather than of five ; and the changes that Gaunt visualized were certainly vastly more leisurely than those which the school had to undergo during the next ten years.

Meanwhile, one of the changes initiated by his predecessor was coming to fruition. On June 18, 1938, Earl Baldwin, who had ceased to be Prime Minister the year before, came to open the Preston Science School. Significant in the history of the College, it was shortly to be of even greater significance in the history of the nation. Coming events were already casting their shadows over that summer's day. Few were the speeches of public men in that year that did not include a comment on the sombre scene in Europe ; and Earl Baldwin's was no exception.

In October 1938 Gaunt reported to the Council that masters were being trained in Air Raid Precautions 'with a view to their being in a position to train boys later'. In November the Editorial of the *Malvernian* said with an air of insouciance, 'It takes more than the imminence of war to unsettle Malvern for any length of time. It is true that a little excitement pervaded the atmosphere ; a few of those over eighteen wandered around, vainly trying to obtain reassurance about the age for joining up ; digging became more than just a dilatory pastime for those bored on Sundays ; but for the most part everything went on just the same. The signing of the Munich agreement was heralded with joy and an extra half-holiday. . . .'

Then in December events began to happen of which the editors of the *Malvernian* were at that time blissfully ignorant. Gaunt has told the war-time story of Malvern in vivid detail in a little book called *Two Exiles*, and all the quotations that follow, unless otherwise acknowledged, are taken from it.

'Following the admirable example of my predecessor, Mr. F. S. Preston,' Gaunt writes, 'I was accustomed in those palmy days of peace to have my correspondence delivered to me together with a cup of tea in my bedroom : a quick glance at the letters followed by a few moments of reflection during the morning toilet often saved valuable time a little later in the day. On Boxing Day, the 26th of December, 1938, among a number of envelopes containing Christmas cards one letter stood out among the rest. It was pale bluish grey, was marked on the outside "Secret and Confidential", and bore the crest of His Majesty's Office of Works on the back of the envelope. Speculating rapidly on what signal honour I was about to be asked to accept, I slit open the envelope. Inside was a second sealed envelope, this time marked "SECRET. To be opened only by H. C. A. Gaunt, Esq., M.A., Headmaster of Malvern College." I complied. It contained a letter from Sir Patrick Duff, Permanent Secretary to the Ministry of Works, informing me that the Government "have had under consideration the question of earmarking a number of large buildings outside London for national purposes in the event of war, and I am afraid it is my ungrateful duty to let you know that Malvern College is one of those earmarked." . . . He stressed that it was essential that what he had told me should remain a close secret. He would authorize me to inform the Chairman of the College Council, but the matter must go no further. . . .

'The need for secrecy was, of course, a most serious hindrance, but it was of the highest importance to the Government, first that it should not be known that plans were being made at all, since war might not break out, and secondly that the nature of the plan should not be known if it did. Secrecy was just as important to us. Had it been widely known that the College would have to move from Malvern, parents and prospective parents would certainly have thought twice before allowing their boys to come : and it is always a bad plan to upset people before it is necessary, especially where a contingency may not arise.'

At an interview in London, Sir Patrick told Gaunt that his department could not help a great deal in obtaining alternative accommodation if the College were taken over. Gaunt was given permission to inform his Second Master, Major Elliott, of what was in the air ; and he sent him off on a discreet search for alternative accommodation. Large hotels in resorts suggested themselves ; but 'the hotels, one and all, told us that they were expecting a large inflow of clients from dangerous areas, to whom they would charge high prices if war came, and that consequently the rent which they would charge us would be very high also, if indeed they were prepared to hand over the hotel. Moreover, they also demanded a high retaining fee. . . . Of course we could not commit the

College to heavy expenditure which might prove to be wholly unnecessary.'

In desperation, Gaunt and S. P. Richardson, the Vice-Chairman of the Council,* went to see Sir Patrick again in April 1939. The interview looked like being completely fruitless. 'After nearly two hours we were no nearer a solution ; so we prepared to withdraw for the time being. At this point Sir Patrick almost casually mentioned that he had that very morning received a letter from the Duke of Marlborough, offering Blenheim Palace to the Government if war should break out ; and he added "But I suppose it would not be large enough for what you want !" ' Of course Gaunt said he would like to see the Palace, and the Duke invited him to come the next day.

After having been shown over the whole Palace by the Duchess of Marlborough and Mr Sacré, the Duke's Estate Agent, Gaunt was vividly aware of the grave deficiencies in the buildings as they stood ; but it would be possible to house and run the school at Blenheim if the need arose ; and the decision to accept the Duke's offer was made swiftly, for hesitation might mean that the Palace would be offered to someone else.

During the months that followed, plans for moving the school to Blenheim were drawn up ; but nothing beyond paper preparations could be made. War was still not certain, and the Duke could hardly permit the Palace to be reconstituted to suit the needs of a school unless war actually occurred. But one vitally important improvement was made to the Palace : 'In June, Lady Sarah Spencer-Churchill, the Duke's eldest daughter, became eighteen and the Duke celebrated the occasion by a Grand Ball to which a thousand guests were invited and which was described by a shrewd commentator as "perhaps the last great European Ball". For

---

* Richardson was empowered to make emergency decisions on behalf of the Council. At Blenheim such decisions had constantly to be made ; so he moved to Woodstock and remained there for as long as the school did.

us this event had more than historical importance, because it gave me assurance that in attempting to cater for 450 boys and staff in the Palace Kitchens and Dining Rooms we were not attempting the impossible ; and the Duke very generously arranged to leave for our possible use the fairly extensive equipment which he had installed in the Kitchens, and which later proved invaluable.'

On September 1, 1939, Poland was invaded. That day Ministry of Works officials arrived at the College to prepare it for the Admiralty in case it was compelled by massive bombing to move from London. Gaunt summoned the staff to Malvern. There began the task of packing and labelling the contents of boarding-houses and the school, although the College was not yet requisitioned and no one was supposed to know that the school might be moving. On September 7 the requisition order was at last served. It was only now that reconstruction at Blenheim and the move from Malvern could begin.

Term was due to start on September 28, three weeks later, and of course had to be postponed ; but it was only by a fortnight, a very short time considering what was done in those thirty-five days under the tireless and incisive leadership of Major Elliott, nobly helped by Mr Hubbard, the College Architect, and Mr Hartree, the Duke's electrician.

First, the moveable treasures of the Palace — a vast quantity of furniture and antiques of all kinds — had to be evacuated and stored by the Blenheim Estate staff. Other treasures — great tapestries and pictures, worth many thousands of pounds — were so difficult to store that the Duke decided that they must stay as they were in their places on the damask walls of the State Rooms. They had to be protected, as had the 200-year-old parquet floor. So a screen of Essex Board had to be erected in front of the pictures (without a nail being driven into walls or floors) ; the parquet had to be covered with linoleum and coconut matting, 2,400 square yards of it ; the eighteenth-century curtains had to be protected with canvas covers ; and pads of felt were fixed to the mahogany doors. The enormous window-space of the Palace had to be provided with black-out : some of the windows in the Great Hall and the Library reached to a height of sixty feet.

Meanwhile the equipment from Malvern was arriving at Blenheim. 'Practically all transport at this time, at any rate in the Midlands, was under Government control, and consequently the services of the local firms were secured for us by the Ministry of Works. This relieved us of one great anxiety, but caused us another, for although we were spared the trouble and expense of securing vans and labour, we had no control over the movements of the vans or the work of the men. We watched with apprehension the loading up, which was carried out at break-neck speed. At Blenheim we had to be ready at all hours of the day to direct the contents as they arrived at the Palace steps to their proper destination, and the final blow came when on the second day the men announced that they had received orders to dump the vanloads on the steps and return to Malvern with the utmost speed. This meant that the whole of the fifty-five vanloads had to be carried bodily, to the places assigned, by members of the Teaching Staff, the Office Staff, the Ground Staff, the Domestic Staff and any others whose services could be obtained, during a period of ten days from breakfast time until dusk.'

In the middle of all this, 'an official at Malvern announced that he had instructions from London to commandeer the whole of our beds and bedding ! It was only after I had myself telephoned the Ministry in London that this order was rescinded.'

The kitchen installations in the Palace ran on petrol gas, which was likely soon to be unobtainable as well as being prohibitive in price. A gas-main therefore had to be laid from the Palace to Woodstock, a distance of about a mile, and a gang of masters began to hack through the limestone to dig a trench for it until a firm with a pneumatic drill could be procured. Boilers, pipes, racks, basins, lighting, ventilation

fans, and a host of other things had to be installed. Sixty
W.C.s were built outside, 'a mushroom growth appearing
out of the setting concrete with the unabashed functionalism
which we are told makes all things beautiful'.[1] Finally,
sixteen large huts were erected in the main court-yard. These
were to provide class-room accommodation, though they
were not finished until three weeks after the boys arrived.
During that time half the boys would go out for walks while
the other half were taught in the dormitories, where an almost
surrealist juxtaposition of iron bedsteads, gowned pedagogues,
and baroque gilt met the eye.

During those same early weeks there were special difficulties
in the kitchens while further apparatus was being installed ;
but eventually there was enough equipment to enable food to
arrive still more or less warm after its long journey from the
kitchens to the Great Hall.

The boys soon became used to living out of the trunks
under the beds and to the other makeshifts that had to be
devised. There were of course changes beyond these material
ones. The authorities aimed to carry on the house traditions at
Blenheim in spite of centralization of housing and feeding ;
but inevitably the Houses meant less under such conditions.
Indeed, some housemasters had perforce to live outside the
Palace and so found it very much more difficult to keep closely
in touch with their boys. But if the 'family' feeling diminished,
the community feeling increased. 'I do not think', writes
Gaunt, 'that in the long run the mixing of the school would
have been as satisfactory as the old system, though we certainly
gained something important from the experiment.'

The boys, too, felt that much had been gained from their
experiences. The Editorial of the first *Malvernian* published
at Blenheim began,

'Few in number must be the editorials penned in a bathroom ; very few in number those penned in a palace ; and
unique must be that penned in the bathroom of a palace. For
the first time therefore in the history of school magazines, we

are in a position to put forward a convincing claim to originality in an editorial. For the bathroom at Blenheim (there are many of them) constitutes a precious oasis of peace and quiet ; and therefore was the environment in which this was penned — pencilled rather, for ink is taboo at Blenheim. We have all by now endured an experience which, whether we have enjoyed it or not, has been of exceptional educational value. And most of us have enjoyed it.'

The awareness of the turmoil and of the crowded conditions was made less acute by the calm beauty and spaciousness of Blenheim Park and the grandiose conception of the Palace itself. These kept breaking through into consciousness. Boys wrote about their 'first glimpse of the beech-girt lake, grey-blue in the early sunlight, its waveless surface gently veined by the fussy paddling of myriad coots ; and those quiet half hours, construing Sophocles astride a leaden sphinx, a dumb creature proud in her impassivity, amid the sunlit splashings and green formality of the lower Terrace'. The view down the long avenue to the Column of Victory at the end of it added to that sense of history to which the nation was being roused. And in the very cold weather during the Lent term, the scenes of skating on the frozen lake while the sun was setting behind a screen of frost-bound trees had a tingling beauty of their own.

But the cold weather brought its own problems. The heating in the huts was not good. Boys came into morning school wrapped in coats and rugs, to find that icicles had formed under the corrugated iron roofs during the night. As the temperature slowly rose, they melted and dripped onto the forms below. (In the summer, with the sun beating down on the roofs, the huts became so hot that the moisture dripped off the boys onto the floor below !) An influenza epidemic broke out. Some of the cases turned into pneumonia. The San Cab which had been brought from Malvern — a great Daimler, with unhygienic hangings and peeling paint-work but with splendidly polished brass and copper fittings —

made many journeys between the Palace and the private house in the Park which had been converted into a Sanatorium. But this house had room for only twenty boys ; and at one time 150 boys were down with influenza. Dr. Elkington himself fell ill, but, though hardly able to stand, continued throughout to attend to his patients.

With the spring came the end of the 'phoney war', and then Dunkirk and the collapse of France. The descendant of the victor of Blenheim became Prime Minister. The Local Defence Volunteers, later known as the Home Guard, came into being ; boys and masters formed contingents which patrolled the grounds at night.* Firewatching on the roofs of the Palace was organized. 'Early in June there suddenly arrived in Blenheim Park a complete Canadian Armoured Division. In twenty-four hours the Park was festooned with camouflage nets over guns, anti-aircraft batteries, armoured cars, lorries and tanks ; while vast spaces were covered with the tents, kitchens, stores and military equipment of six thousand men. For ten days this occupation lasted, during which time we entertained some five hundred men to a great open air concert on the Palace steps, and a number of boys learned to play Baseball. Then one evening the division began packing up, and by early morning the men were gone, leaving behind them hardly a trace of their invasion.'

At Blenheim, as throughout England, people that summer felt the contrast between the grim events in Europe and one of the most beautiful summers of the century. Cricket on the Great Lawn and swimming in the Lake all took place under the same blue sky out of which, in France, the Stukas were swooping on columns of refugees. Even more incongruous it must have been that at this moment of crisis in the nation's affairs, the school could return to its home in Malvern.

It will be recalled that Malvern had been commandeered

---

* In August two Malvern boys on holiday on the outskirts of South London were on duty with the local Home Guard platoon and helped to bring down a German raider with concentrated rifle fire.

MALVERN AT BLENHEIM

to house the Admiralty in case London were so heavily bombed that the efficient conduct of the war from Whitehall became impossible. In that case 'the First Lord of the Admiralty, then Mr Churchill himself, would have occupied the School House Drawing Room as his private office, and the Preston Science School would have served as the chief Signal Station for our fleet and merchant men all over the Seven Seas'. But the period of the 'phoney war' had given the Admiralty time to build and equip vast underground shelters in London as well as a mass of hutments at Malvern which would enable it to return the College to its owners in September. It still wanted to keep some of the school's buildings for its own purposes, notably the houses on the North side of the grounds, Nos. 1, 2 and 5, to house some of the personnel of H.M.S. *Duke*. This was the name given to a conglomeration of buildings which had been put up on the southern end of the football fields and which was an Initial Training Centre for the Navy. Certain other buildings — the Main College Buildings, the Pavilion Block, the Monastery, the Museum, the Grub Shop, and the Porter's Lodge — were returned on the understanding that they might be required at forty-eight hours' notice if a crash evacuation of the Admiralty from London had to take place before all the new hutments were completed at the end of October. The temporary loss of the three North Houses was not a serious matter. Since the school was so depleted in numbers, it could only help to have them occupied by a rent-paying Government Department ; and if the worst came to the worst and the crash evacuation did take place, the school could manage in the houses that remained to it for the few weeks until the hutments were completed. In March 1940, therefore, Gaunt had been able to announce that the school would return to Malvern in September.

And so at the end of the summer term, Malvern said good-bye to Blenheim and the Duke and Duchess of Marlborough. The Duke and his family had lived in the private wing of the

Palace all the time and had always shown the greatest interest in the school. He had turned the old Riding School into an Assembly Hall and Gymnasium and had told the boys they could use the fine model railway in the Orangerie if they got it working, which they soon did. He had entertained some members of the staff and some of the senior boys ; and his friendly and hospitable attitude was reflected by all the members of his Estate staff, too. At the end of the stay at Blenheim, there was a little ceremony. All the boys had autographed a book which was given to the Duchess ; and the Duke made a speech in which he thanked them for not having broken up the place — 'and it's quite true : we didn't', marvels one O.M. when he reflects on how careless boys in the mass normally are about their surroundings.

The school returned to a Malvern that was very different from the sleepy little town it had been before the war. 'I doubt whether many other towns, outside London, contained so great a variety of men and women of different countries meeting frequently together. In the College itself, at No. 5, there were the Free French Cadets ; a contingent of the Belgian Army had its headquarters at the Abbey Hotel ; the Records Branch of the Polish Navy and a small contingent of Greeks were in the town ; and on occasions we had visitors from Yugo-Slavia, Norway, and Holland at some of the dances and parties which were held. For a short while a contingent of Canadians were at the Malvern House Hotel, while Americans and Australians were frequent visitors. . . . Our own English soldiers were of course much in evidence ; there was a wing of the R.A.F. at Pale Manor, while the new Admiralty buildings were by early 1941 occupied by H.M.S. *Duke*, a Naval Initial Training Centre. Their Officers' Mess was at No. 2 and in Prior's Mount, and we saw a good deal of them, especially as they also used the Gymnasium and Swimming Baths from time to time.'

The Free French Cadets, to whom Gaunt referred in this passage, were some French boys who had cycled to the coast when the Germans invaded France, and had made good their escape. They were some 200 ; and the Free French Army in England wanted to train about fifty of them for commissions. Gaunt was asked whether Malvern could accommodate them ; the Ministry of Works released No. 5, and the French boys arrived in January 1941. Their red walking-out cloaks were soon a familiar sight, and the school saw a good deal of them, for they used class-rooms, the Gym, and the playing fields. They took part in the School Sports in March and joined a number of other activities. General De Gaulle came to inspect them in September 1941, unfortunately when the school was on holiday. Thirty-five of the sixty-three who had been trained at Malvern later died when they returned to France with the Army of Liberation and led the newly-raised, en-thusiastic, but untrained militia into battle. A memorial seat stands outside No. 5 today. It was unveiled in 1949.

Meanwhile the Malvern House System got back into its stride, though with some important modifications. The boys of Nos. 1, 2, and 5 combined with Nos. 8, 6, and 7 respectively. And an important change in the position of housemasters had taken place at Blenheim. With central feeding and accom-modation, it had clearly been impossible for housemasters to run their houses as a private commercial proposition, as they had done ever since the school was founded. In 1940 the College had assumed financial responsibility. The house-masters surrendered their boarding fees to the College and were paid salaries instead. Originally devised as a temporary solution for the period while the school was at Blenheim, abandoned on the return to Malvern in September 1940, this arrangement was reintroduced at Harrow and officially became permanent in 1943. The old system had originated during a period when economic conditions were relatively stable. Bearing in mind the Depression in the 1930s and the rising prices in the 1940s and since, it is not difficult to imagine that housemasters were only too glad to be relieved of acute personal financial cares which their nineteenth-century predecessors had rarely experienced. Nor had these earlier housemasters had to worry very much about domestic help, a problem which during the war and afterwards became increasingly serious and which from 1959 onwards was to compel more and more houses to turn to outside caterers who, with their pool of domestic staff, were able to avoid the recurrent crises when cooks and kitchen helps left at the shortest notice.

The financial responsibility for the houses was now added to the Council's many other worries. Even before the war broke out, numbers had been declining again ; and not only at Malvern. Early in 1939 the Headmasters' Conference had prepared a report on 'The Decline in the School Population and its Effects upon the Public Schools'.* By that time the numbers at Malvern were down to 430, which was much below the lowest point that had been reached while the Depression was at its worst six years before. Then the evacuation to Blenheim produced a further decline — not because many boys were taken away,† but because the entries diminished under those circumstances. The year at Blenheim began with 398 boys, and when the College returned to Malvern a year later, it was only 357 strong. Some of this loss could undoubtedly be ascribed to a loss of what business enterprises call goodwill. The Government paid compensation for the physical move to Blenheim, for physical damage and structural alterations, and also paid rent for the buildings in Malvern on a scale that enabled the College to pay the rent of Blenheim Palace ; but the Government could not possibly pay com-

---

* It accounted for the decline in the school population in this way : 'For some short time after the (first) war the birthrate rose ; since then it has fallen. . . . In the immediate future a further fall in the boy population is a matter of certainty ; and looking forward over the next twenty years, it is evident that the schools will have to face a period of contraction.' Yet by 1959 most public schools were full to capacity.

† Only six boys already at the school were withdrawn because of the move to Blenheim, and only seven when the school went to Harrow. One of the Junior Chapel Prefects on the Hill was in fact a former Harrovian whom his parents had taken away from Harrow in 1940 and sent to Malvern for greater safety !

pensation for loss of goodwill, since legislation could not be devised to cover such undefinable sums. In this case, for example, it would be impossible to say exactly how much of the decline was due to the continuation of a trend which had set in before the war and how much was due to the requisition. The return to Malvern did not arrest the trend. Before the second evacuation in April 1942, numbers had fallen by another score to 336, when the buildings which at that time were still available to the school could have accommodated 400 boarders. In the summer of 1941 the Council Minutes go as far as to say that 'if numbers of boys in the future were to fall seriously, it might be thought expedient to explore the possibilities of amalgamating with another school'. The Council could hardly have anticipated how absurdly cautious that phraseology was to appear nine months later.

Worrying though these problems were, at least the daily life of the school was able to return to more normal conditions than had prevailed at Blenheim. It is true that it was still very different from what it had been before the war. As in the First World War, the Corps now paraded twice a week. The War Office introduced a new Certificate 'A' syllabus whose more rigorous requirements of physical fitness could only be met by much more serious training. The Air Training Corps was formed early in 1941.* The Youth Service Corps was set up. This was a body whose members undertook to spend at least two hours a week doing certain kinds of work like collecting salvage, working in canteens, and a whole host of other chores that would release adult labour. It began as a voluntary organization which 200 boys joined. In the course of time it became in practice compulsory and continued its activities in the school grounds long after the end of the war.

The school did a good deal of agricultural work, under the guidance of F. W. Roberts. Part of the Firs Field and some land beyond No. 7 was broken up and laid out in plots for a vegetable garden. Each house in turn gave up games one day

* The Naval Section was started after the war, in 1952.

a week and held itself at the disposal of the garden. It was not very skilful work at first, and Roberts himself, 'though buoyed up by thoughts of national emergency, became very conscious of his strictly amateur status in matters gardening'.[4] Certainly not everyone who farmed was seized with a love of the soil ; not, for instance, the author of this little poem in the *Malvernian* of March 1942 :

> There is a tide in the affairs of men
> That ebbs and flows, and ebbs and flows again.
> Of ebbs, the lowest of the very low
> Is weeding, hoeing, picking things that grow.
> The themes of this unhappy little dirge
> Are buckets without bottoms, and an urge
> Which always grips one when in throes of toil,
> To throw those lovely, sticky lumps of soil
> At someone's head : potatoes for that matter
> Fly very well, and fortunately shatter
> On striking their objective : otherwise
> The effect of hits would be beyond surmise.

There was tractor driving on the football fields ; and the school also did a lot of work at agricultural camps, not only in the holidays, but in term-time, too. Each side of the school was sent off in turn for a week's work at such a camp at Evesham.

Then the introduction of clothes-rationing brought changes in what had been perhaps one of the most clothes-conscious public schools in England. Grey shirts with collars attached replaced white ones on weekdays ; and in 1941 Gaunt devised a new school uniform which would cost only thirteen clothing coupons instead of twenty-six. It would consist of 'a fawn windproof and waterproof jacket, with corduroy shorts and woollen stockings of similar colour'. The boys cheerfully put up with much during the war ; but this was going too far. The new uniform never caught on and disappeared altogether at Harrow.

As far as Malvern was concerned, the story of the evacuation to Harrow began on April 25, 1942. On that day some government inspectors arrived, spent two hours on a hurried inspection of the empty buildings (it was a week before the beginning of the summer term), and then left without giving any reason for their visit. Gaunt was sufficiently disturbed to go to London immediately to see the Ministry of Works, though he could hardly believe that Malvern would be subjected to a second evacuation. At the Ministry 'I began by apologizing for troubling them over what might be a silly scare, and until that very moment I was half expecting to be walking out of the building ten minutes later with a sense of having been idiotically disturbed by the whole affair, but with a happy reassurance in my mind once again. . . . I need not have troubled to apologize : within two minutes it became obvious that the situation was extremely critical, if not already past repair. I was told that owing to an unexpected development in the course of the War a certain vital Government Department had been compelled to move their establishment elsewhere immediately ; that this was a War Cabinet decision and that Malvern College had been selected as the most suitable premises in the country.' The Ministry of Works and the Board of Education were making the most strenuous efforts to stop this second requisition. Mr Butler himself (then President of the Board of Education) would be pleading the cause of Malvern at a special committee which the Cabinet had set up under Sir John Anderson, the Lord President of the Council (whose son, incidentally, had been at Malvern in the 1920s). The Committee would be meeting in two days' time. When it did, Mr Butler's advocacy was unavailing ; and on April 30 Gaunt went to London again to hear for the first time what exactly was the nature of this sudden emergency that compelled the Government to take over the College.

Earlier that month there had been a special commando raid on Bruneval, on the French coast, where the German Radar station was situated. Among the information that was captured there were plans for a heavy attack by aircraft and seventeen trainloads of parachute troops during the next full moon on the Telecommunications Research Establishment at Swanage. This establishment was concerned with all the work on Radar and was of absolutely vital importance. The Prime Minister had given orders that T.R.E. must move away from the south coast before the next full moon.

'T.R.E. needed certain special geographical features for their work, including fairly high hills, a wide range of vision, proximity to an aerodrome * and, of course, a secluded place of comparative safety. In addition there must be buildings which could be very speedily converted into the laboratories and workshops which were needed and ground on which new buildings could be built. A large school or institution was clearly suitable, provided that it were in the right place and the Ministry of Aircraft Production authorities, under whose auspices T.R.E. worked, at once consulted the Board of Education. Of all the schools in England two were pre-eminently suitable, Marlborough and Malvern ; and of the two Malvern was preferred : for investigation quickly showed that the town drainage system at Marlborough was barely adequate for the present inhabitants and would be quite inadequate for the increased population which T.R.E. would bring and for the special scientific work in which they were engaged.' Besides, the City of London School had been evacuated to Marlborough, so that requisition there would mean displacing two schools instead of one, as at Malvern.

So there it was. Now of course came the problem of finding alternative accommodation. The Ministry of Works had already told Gaunt that it had a complete schedule of all large buildings throughout the country ; that only one of these — Berkeley Castle in Gloucestershire — was unoccupied, but that it had no proper water supply. A half-built Canadian Camp near Hereford had been inspected on April 29 ; but,

* The aerodrome at Defford was to be used in conjunction with T.R.E.'s work.

apart from being unfinished, it was impossible on other grounds too. It looked very much as if the College might have to be dispersed by Houses among such other schools as could take them ; and now, on April 30th, an afternoon of telephoning from the Board of Education brought generous responses from several Headmasters. Had this dispersal taken place, that might well have been the end of the history of Malvern College. Its identity could hardly have been maintained, and it is doubtful whether the school could have brought sufficient pressure on the Government after the war to secure a sufficiently early release of its buildings.

But there was one other avenue to be explored. At a housemasters' meeting during those days, someone had remarked that Harrow School was considerably depleted as a result of its nearness to London and might be able to take three or four houses, or, possibly, even the whole school. After testing out the reactions of some parents to the idea of moving the school so near London and getting a positive response on that score, Gaunt on May 1 telephoned Mr A. P. Boissier, the acting headmaster of Harrow.* 'I outlined briefly the facts of our requisition ; I made plain the plight we were in ; I asked whether it were possible for Harrow to accommodate one or two of our houses or even the whole School ; and I ended with the words, "Can you do anything for us ?" He had listened to my recital in silence, and his reply was brief, "I think so ; come and have lunch !" How characteristic of the man those words were I was to learn later.' That afternoon, May 1, Gaunt and Boissier made plans in the latter's study. 'The study was not especially remarkable, except that, as he sat at his desk facing the window, there was behind him a small cupboard fixed to the walls. On the inside of the doors of this were fixed lists of the Staff and their telephone numbers and innumerable other pieces of reference which a Headmaster must have constantly at hand. Mr Boissier had only to open the cupboard doors to find what he wanted, and

* The Headmaster, P. C. Vellacott, was on war service.

he did this almost automatically without interrupting the flow of conversation. This constant opening and shutting is one of my most abiding memories during these hectic days, for it signified consultation, decision, and action of a remarkable kind and of amazing speed.'

Boissier said he could eventually offer Malvern five houses ; but of these only one, Rendalls, was actually vacant at that time. The Coldstream Guards were in Westacre ; the Ministry of Health had a hospital in Newlands ; a London Insurance Company had rented Deyncourt as temporary offices during the blitz period ; and though Harrow would be willing to move its boys out of Bradby's and put them into other houses, this could not be done at once since it was right at the beginning of term. (The beginning of the Malvern term had of course been postponed by telegram. The school reassembled at Harrow on May 28.)

Mr Butler had promised to do what he could to get the Harrow premises vacated by the government departments and even by the Insurance Company, and within a few days they were. But the Deyncourt kitchens had been converted into an air-raid shelter ; and this led to the renting of Tower House, a private house nearby, to afford a dining hall, a kitchen, and more accommodation for Deyncourt.

The move to Harrow of course meant further amalgamation of the Malvern Houses. F. W. Roberts offered to surrender the housemastership of 1/8 and F. H. Hooper that of No. 9. (Hooper as Second Master was a rock of strength to the school throughout the years at Harrow and for some time afterwards.) In the next few years, Houses were referred to by the name of their housemasters. No. 3 in Rendall's was Cosgrove's ; No. 4 in Westacre was Chadder's ; No. 5/7 in Deyncourt was Colthurst's ; No. 2/6 in Newlands was Salter's. The School House boys were, to start with, dispersed in small groups in the Harrow Houses until Harrow could free Bradby's. Gaunt's work as a headmaster had become so heavy that he gave up School House to D. W.

Erskine. So ended the long tradition by which the headmaster had always been a housemaster too.

While the Houses were thus being allocated, processions of vans were again on their way from Malvern. The urgency to clear Malvern for the T.R.E. was, if anything, even greater than it had been in the case of the Admiralty two and a half years before ; and the chaos at the Malvern end was infinitely worse because at the same time another procession of vans was arriving there with the T.R.E. equipment from Swanage. There was a welter of contradictory orders from one official after another. Major Elliott and the Bursar, Mr Ker, not only had to arrange for the College property to be moved (not necessarily straight to Harrow, since the railways could not cope with the thirty-eight railway containers all at once), but had also to make an inventory of everything that went and everything that stayed behind, for purposes of compensation.

At the same time builders were swarming all over the College grounds which, with astonishing speed, began to sprout new buildings on every available open space except the Senior Turf. At the same time the houses were transformed. All but three were converted into laboratories and workshops. Wooden partitions disappeared — that was the end of the cubicles in the dormitories of most of the Houses—, hundreds of miles of new wiring were installed, 'the entire heating systems of the Houses and of the Main Buildings were scrapped and more powerful ones installed throughout, complete with new boilers and brick boiler-houses. Girders were erected in many places to strengthen floors, A.R.P. installations and emergency water tanks appeared, blastproof walls were built, three electric power stations were installed. Within six weeks a huge steel-girdered workshop with 14″ brick walls had been roofed and equipped, and a large canteen capable of feeding 1,500 people at least at one sitting had been completed, the whole of the grass space between the Science Schools and No. 3 was bristling with huts, and in many parts of the grounds strange buildings of a special design rose up.'

If the activity at Harrow was not on such a gigantic scale, it was nevertheless hectic enough ; and the only way of keeping pace with the arrival of the vans when some of the houses were not ready to receive any furniture was to unload everything into Westacre, which was filled from top to bottom with equipment which then gradually had to be redistributed. But on May 28 Malvern was ready to begin a new phase of its existence which was to last for nearly four and a half years.

Drastic and sudden upheavals of the kind that Malvern twice underwent necessarily bulk large in the history of a school. Those who took part in them remember with a kind of awe 'what feats they did that day' and of what exertions and achievements they were capable at a time of crisis. When set against decades of peace-time routine, the story of these years takes on something of the character of a saga. But when it is set against the much greater exertions and tribulations which others suffer in time of war, legitimate pride should be tempered by great humility. Gaunt struck that note in his address in Harrow Chapel when the school reassembled :

'Let us consider this catastrophe in its right perspective, against the broader background of the war. Compare our sufferings with the perils and privations which our brothers are facing on land, on sea, and in the air. Consider the lives of those who fought at Singapore or who withdrew fighting week by week along the roads of Burma. Picture for a moment what our allies have to face in France and Poland and Greece. In the larger picture of the war our sufferings and difficulties seem a small part.

'But if against the vast canvas they seem a small part, they are not an insignificant part. I am sure that when the whole story of our evacuation can be told — and it cannot be told now — Malvern College will be found to have played an honourable and vital part in the winning of the war.'

It was the intention both of Malvern and of Harrow that the two schools should retain their separate identities. There was, for example, never any amalgamation of the teaching or of the games. On the other hand, there were other activities and facilities which were shared, and especially at the beginning, when both schools were still very reduced in numbers. Malvern and Harrow School Prefects and School Monitors, for example, had equal authority over members of both schools at first, though this did not last.* There were joint chapel services, the Malvern form of service being adopted for Matins and the Harrow form for Evensong ; but this, too, stopped when the growing numbers could no longer be accommodated together in chapel. The schools shared the Sanatorium, the Tea Shop, and the Library ; and their Choral Societies were joined under Mr Havergal, the Harrow music master, because Julius Harrison, who had succeeded Davison, was unable to come to Harrow. In a few small ways, Malvern had to fit in with Harrow customs. Masters, for example, were 'capped' by the boys rather than greeted in the Malvern fashion to which they reverted again at the end of the war. A custom which was abandoned for good was that of swimming in the nude ; not, according to one correspondent, because Harrow protested, but because women who worked in a N.A.A.F.I. near the Ducker objected to coming across naked sunbathers. When, back at Malvern, an outbreak of pink eye among the boys in 1951 was attributed to the fine fluff from the bathing trunks in the water, the authorities tried to revert to the old custom ; but the school prefects expressed such strong objections on behalf of the whole school that the plan was abandoned.

In the heat of occasional ducker fights and snow fights, relations between the boys of the two schools might some-times become a little less than friendly ; but in general the harmony on the Hill was well maintained throughout the evacuation, and Malvern owes a great debt of gratitude to Harrow for its friendly and cooperative hospitality. 'But for the decisive action of great-hearted Harrovians in those critical

* *The Harrovian*, a weekly publication, reduced to a single sheet by war-time paper-shortage, gave space to lists of Malvern school prefects.

days of 1942 Malvern would not be counted among the Public Schools today', writes Gaunt. 'But the early sense of adventure and the first flush of generosity and self-sacrifice easily pall when the weeks lengthen into months and the months to years. Moreover, Mr Boissier, when he retired in September 1942, left to his successor a legacy not of the latter's choosing, and one which no Headmaster would have wished to inherit. Yet Mr Moore, in adopting the legacy of his predecessor, had also assumed his mantle. Throughout our whole time of evacuation to Harrow we have been fortified by the knowledge that come what might we should not be let down.'

An Editorial of the *Malvernian* at Harrow suggested that 'Perhaps we appreciate at Harrow more keenly than we did at Malvern the urgency of the war'. Not that the school magazine contained many references to the war as such. The First World War had been far more prolific in letters from the front, and the mood of the school (as of the nation as a whole) was altogether different : the participation of civilians in the second war was less vicarious and therefore perhaps they commented less. But Harrow was nearer London. The air-raid sirens, which had sounded only twice at Blenheim, were heard much more frequently now ; and on February 22, 1944, incendiary bombs dropped on the Harrow School buildings and were put out by the fire-watching teams before they could do any serious damage except to the tea-shop.* And in the second term on the Hill 'the Prime Minister visited Harrow, making our thoughts turn, by his very presence, to the greater world that lies outside our school life.' ³ Speaking to his old school, with a large number of Malvern boys also present, Churchill said,

'You have visitors here now in the shape of a sister school —Malvern. I must say I think this is a very fine affair — to

---

* A gaily written account of that night's events is printed in *The Harrovian* of April 5, 1944. Security regulations account for the time-lag between the raid and the publication of details.

meet the needs of war, to join forces, to share alike, like two regiments that serve side by side in some famous brigade and never forget it for a hundred years after. I was very sorry that I myself had to be responsible for giving some instructions in regard to one of our establishments which made it necessary to take over Malvern at comparatively short notice. But everybody at the School will, I know, make it his business to let their friends and guests carry away with them a memory which will make its mark definitely on the relationship of the two schools — and no doubt to give them a beating in any of the games which you play.'

Mr Butler agreed to come to Malvern's first prize-giving on the Hill, in July 1942 ; and Gaunt writes, 'Mr Butler's willingness to accept this invitation at what must have been one of the busiest times of his life (so far) was most deeply appreciated, for it not only confirmed the debt which we owed to him, but also signified to the world at large that the prosperity of Malvern was treated with real concern by the Government even amid the more serious affairs of 1942'. Herbert Morrison, then Home Secretary, came to speak to the school in February 1944 ; and all these glimpses of men who were at the centre of the great events of the time gave these events an even greater sense of immediacy than they might perhaps have had in quiet Worcestershire.

It was of course easier for busy men to come over to Harrow for an evening than it would have been to travel to Malvern ; and Gaunt took full advantage of the school's proximity to London. He formed a Discussion Society which he invited distinguished men from various walks of life to address. Boys were also able to go to London more frequently, not only for educational and cultural purposes, but also, for instance, to visit the Dockland Settlement, of which Captain Tinton had become Warden in succession to Sir Reginald Kennedy-Cox in 1938. Dockland had of course suffered terribly during the Blitz. Three of the Settlements were a total loss ; and in addition they were desperately short of staff. Twenty boys went to help the Mission in the summer holidays of 1942.

Other boys spent the summer holidays farming, no longer at Evesham, but at Mr Holland-Martin's farm at Overbury, near Tewkesbury. C. B. Lace took on the organization of these Overbury Camps which were to be a feature of Malvern life from 1942 to 1949. The camp, as the *Malvernian* pointed out, was 'on the side of Bredon Hill, and once again we could see the Malvern Hills'. This comment struck a note of nostalgia which was heard far more insistently at Harrow than it had been at Blenheim. As the Headboy of Harrow said compassionately in the Latin Oration to the Harrow Governors:

Nescio qua natale solum dulcedine mentem
Tangit, et immemorem non sinit esse sui.*

Expressed first in visual terms, in a longing for a view of the Malvern Hills and the Severn Valley, this nostalgia presently changed its character. As the years passed, more and more boys came who had never known the ways of the College at Malvern. When the school eventually did go back, there were only four boys who had been at the school before its move to Harrow. And so an anxiety began to be expressed in the *Malvernian* lest certain traditions should be lost. The school prefects who had spent the greater part of their school days at Malvern were always very tradition-conscious. An entry in their Minute Book in Preston's last term reads as follows, 'Heads of Houses met in the School Prefects' Room to discuss the possibility of standardizing privileges throughout the school. This was voted "a good thing", especially if we could set to work and reach a solution definitely before Mr. Gaunt came' — and there followed a summary of the many little ways in which boys establish a hierarchy among themselves : the right to walk about with one hand in your pocket (except when passing School Prefects) if you had been

* 'A man's native soil has for him a kind of attraction, and never allows him to forget it.' The quotation is from Ovid.

T.R.E. AT MALVERN

at the School one year, and to have both hands in your pockets after two years ; the right to sport a white handkerchief in your breastpocket after three years and to wear floral decorations after four ; the right to wear pointed instead of rounded collars after eight terms or on being awarded a First Eleven Colour ; * rules about who was allowed to carry an umbrella or to leave his coat unbuttoned — exalted privileges, these — and a host of other sartorial regulations. Then, when the College went to Harrow, the Head of School wrote down a list of 116 customs which the school had observed at Malvern, many of which could not be observed on the Hill.

One might think that even so, these customs would mean little to boys who had spent the greater part of their school life at Harrow ; and a reading of the Prefects' Minute Book towards the end of the war does in fact suggest that in their anxiety about the loss of traditions they took their lead from what the Headmaster said to them. Gaunt was not by temperament or conviction a conservative ; but after the turmoil and changes of two exiles, he was looking longingly for the stability which old-established traditions might give. So, from 1943 to 1946, successive numbers of the *Malvernian* printed accounts of school customs. They were mostly rules about fagging and rules about dress ; the rule that School House had the sole use of the path leading down from their yard to the Armoury and Pavilion ; that No. 1 did not subject the new boys at the end of their first fortnight to the rather terrifying ordeal that took place in other houses of being examined by the prefects on the customs and slang of the school, but instead made new boys stand on a table and sing a song ; that No. 6 inherited from Toppin's day the privilege of sitting on the Senior itself instead of on the bank to watch matches ; that on command of the Head of House, No. 8 would go for a walk round the garden just before

---

* When it became difficult to get rounded collars and this particular regulation ceased to be a school rule, two houses still maintained the old tradition successfully for another two years.

bed-time on fine summer evenings ; that No. 9 considered it a tradition to have only O.M. housemasters, that it enjoyed sole use of the Monastery garden and was the only house to frown on 'house-bangs' (the banging of spoons, etc., on the table to celebrate the official announcement at supper that a cup had been won).

After the house rules, it was the turn of the school rules. The Editorial of March 1946 urged that all boys should familiarize themselves with these rules before the return to Malvern later that year. 'There should be no necessity for some unsuspecting member of the Lower School to be told off for walking up the main steps and past St. George. On the first Sunday of the new term, everyone should know that the whole School waits in Houses on the Terrace before morning Chapel. No boy should walk past the Masters' Common Room with his hands in his pockets. No one should be ignorant of the traditions and privileges of the seniors. All should know that only members of the Eleven and School Prefects may walk across the Senior ; that in the summer term the whole School walks twice round the Senior after evening Chapel ; that during matches the School sit in Houses on the bank, with the Seniors at the top and Juniors at the bottom.'

The following term, the correspondence column carried two letters, one ironical and one scathing about this solemn recital. In particular the question was raised why a young boy in the Eleven should be given senior privileges which were denied to a young boy in the Sixth Form. But in the same issue a well-known O.M. cricketer threw the weight of his prestige heavily on the other side : 'I am one of the many many old boys who hope desperately that the new Malvern will do its best to reach back over the last few ghastly years and try to touch the unseen hand that guided the School before its days of exile.' And this in turn elicited in the next issue the retort, 'May Malvern be restored home purged of bad traditions, enriched by new traditions. A tradition must stand or fall by itself. If it is backed by sound reason, then it will live ;

but if it needs reactionary propping up by people no longer at the School, then it deserves to die.'

When this letter was written, the school was already back at Malvern. The war was over. 258 Old Malvernians had lost their lives. They are commemorated on the Roll of Honour in the Ante-Chapel. Three of the thirteen masters who had been called up were killed : Gerry Chalk, who had been in charge of Malvern cricket from 1935 to 1937 and had then left to become Captain of Kent ;* A. M. McClure, whose arrival at the College in 1938 had galvanized the Art School ; and H. B. E. Mills.

The school's legal contract with Harrow provided that Malvern's stay there should end within twelve months of the cessation of hostilities with Germany. Not the least of the debts that Malvern owes to Harrow was that the latter did not insist on the letter of the contract being fulfilled when it became clear that T.R.E. would take a good deal longer than that to move. This was a real sacrifice on the part of Harrow, since it had already been compelled to turn away boys who wanted to come to the school, and now had to do so for a further period at a time when the slump in numbers was ending in all schools. (Malvern, whose numbers were down to 268 in January 1944, reopened in Worcestershire with more boys — 402 — than it had had at any time since the beginning of the war.)

The Ministry of Education had promised that Malvern could go back by September 1945 ; but T.R.E. showed little sign of moving, and in the end it needed a question in the House of Commons from Major Conant and subsequent exertions from Ellen Wilkinson, the Minister of Education, to get at least a partial derequisition, enough to enable Malvern to return in September 1946. 'For a term or two,' said Gaunt, 'the scientists of T.R.E. will be working in the College grounds, in nearly all the temporary buildings which they have erected and in some of the College buildings. We shall have to put up with the minimum of redecoration, with such

* He had married the daughter of G. N. Foster.

things as open dormitories, and even with unpartitioned studies for the time being. . . . But we shall be back at last — back to our own home and familiar surroundings — back to the open hills — back, pray God, for good !'

Already before that time, some Malvern boys had had their first glimpse of their school in Worcestershire. During the Overbury Harvest Camp of 1945, 'T.R.E. allowed a party of boys to visit the College grounds. When we arrived at the main gate, we were met by a security officer who was to show us round. A few of us, of course, needed no directing, but the majority were complete strangers to the place. We first went over the School buildings and were allowed into some of the rooms, notably the Sixth Form Room, which is being used as the Superintendent's study. Next we went into the Chapel and were convinced that our memories of its beauty were not exaggerated. . . . We were not allowed into any of the Houses, but from the outside, at least, they looked the same as ever. When we reached the Senior, the members of the Cricket XI present, in defiance of all notices, walked onto it, but a policeman soon turned them off. The wicket was in quite good repair, but the outfield badly needed cutting. . . . Everywhere we went, we encountered police-men, very odd bits of apparatus, and miles of barbed wire. . . . We were all very grateful to the Superintendent for allowing us to go "home" for an hour.' 4

The Superintendent was Mr (as he then was) A. P. Rowe. It was in fact he who had had to make the recommendation that Malvern would be more suitable for T.R.E.'s purposes than Marlborough. After a distinguished career as head of T.R.E. and then Vice-Chancellor of Adelaide University, he retired to Malvern in 1958 and wrote to the Headmaster that if by doing some teaching, he could make up for some of the difficulties he had been compelled to cause the College during the war, he would be glad to do so. His wisdom and wide view of the world have greatly enriched the life of the school ; and the Rowe Room in the new research block of the science buildings marks the school's respect for his connection with Malvern in war and in peace.

In 1948 Dr Rowe published a little book, *One Story of Radar*, which gives an excellent account of the war-time work that was going on in the grounds of the College. He describes the physical transformation of the grounds. Only the Senior Turf remained sacrosanct throughout the war, a touch which is as characteristically English as is the atmosphere in which it was possible to have 'a row of Air Vice-Marshals and Air Commodores sitting at the feet of flannel-bagged lecturers' in the Radar School in the Monastery.[5] The panelled Sixth Form class-room, which T.R.E. had promised not to convert into a laboratory, was not only the Chief Superintendent's office, but also the scene of the famous 'Sunday Soviets' — meetings of scientists, university dons, civil servants, service officers, and occasionally even Cabinet Ministers, at which high matters of policy and priority were discussed. Big School was used for demonstrating a sample of almost every radar-training device to visiting service chiefs and Ministers and to King George VI and Queen Elizabeth when they came on July 19, 1944. The Gymnasium had been turned into a store house, the Memorial Library into a Drawing Office, Nos. 5 and 9 into hostels, and the other houses into laboratories. 'From almost every College window overlooking the Vale of Evesham could be seen the metal mirrors associated with centimetre radar.'[6] Work on the application of centimetre radar, the most dramatic weapon in the whole radar arsenal, was done in the Preston Science School and in No. 8.

Most of the really decisive theoretical discoveries had been made at Swanage ; but Malvern saw their development and application. Moreover, the early use of radar had been largely defensive : the identification of hostile aircraft or shipping, first from the ground and then later from the air, so that night-fighters could home onto night-bombers and coastal command aircraft could begin to spot submarines under certain conditions. The work at Malvern was mainly offensive.

Among the devices which were developed now were 'Oboe', which made possible high precision bombing or the accurate flare-dropping of the Pathfinder Force ; 'H₂S', which gave bombers accurate radar pictures of the towns beneath them and therefore made possible the bomber offensive which began in February 1943 and brought the war home to Berlin itself in November that year ; 'Window', the strips of metallized paper which confused the German radar system ; the various devices which spelt the end of the U-boat menace and compelled Hitler to announce on the radio in the summer of 1943 that 'the temporary setback to our U-boats is due to one single technical invention of our enemies' ; 'Gee', which guided the armada of large and small ships onto the beaches of Normandy in all weathers and which made one naval officer say that that misty day in June 1944 should be called Gee-Day rather than D-Day ; 'Eureka' and 'Rebecca', devices by which the first parachute detachment to be dropped could guide the following troop-carrying aircraft to drop their detachments close to the first.* No sooner had one technique been perfected than the scientists set to work on what would replace it when the Germans had discovered, as they were bound to do in time, how to counter the new inventions. In this way Britain retained the initiative in the scientific field and bought valuable time, so that when the Germans came to develop their revolutionary weapons, the V.1 and V.2, it was too late. The claim that the Second World War was won on the playing-fields of Malvern may be exaggerated ; but it contains an element of truth.†

* Work on 'Oboe' and 'H₂S' was done in the Preston Laboratories ; on 'Window' and other counter-measures in No. 7 ; on 'Eureka' and 'Rebecca' in No. 2. The Ground Radar Equipment for D-Day was developed in School House. Work on aerials was done in No. 3. From No. 4 liaison with Bomber, Coastal, and Fighter Commands was maintained ; and the scientists who observed how the equipment was actually working in ships and aircraft reported back to the centre in No. 6. The administration was housed in No. 1.

† When after the war a film called *Top Secret* was made about the story of radar, Malvern College had to suffer the indignity of appearing in it under the name of 'Kippenhampton College' !

When T.R.E. eventually left Malvern College, it did not move far away. It took over the buildings of H.M.S. *Duke*, the naval training centre which, it will be recalled, had been erected on the southern end of the football fields. The Malvernian Society now sold this ground to the Government for a sum which enabled it to buy eleven acres contiguous to the rest of the field. Today the uncompromisingly rectangular buildings of the R.R.E.* and of the Chase School which was opened near by in 1953 have somewhat altered the view from the College towards Bredon ; though even with this obstacle, it is still one of the loveliest views that any boy in England can have from his school.

The satisfaction of the return home was enhanced by the expansion in entries to which reference has already been made. Numbers went up by over 100 in the first two years back at Malvern. In the following year, entries exceeded vacancies, and numbers continued to rise for the next two years after that. The increase was badly needed, for there was a very large overdraft at the bank until the payment of government compensation — amounting to £150,000 in all — had been completed in 1952 ; and even then the College's overdraft still amounted to £28,000.

The immediate post-war years were in addition a period of rapidly rising costs which quickly wiped out the extra income derived from frequent increases in fees — these rose from £180 a year in September 1946 to £276 a year in September 1953. The Malvernian Society as ever did what it could to help ; and in particular paid large sums for the repair of various College buildings. It also bought 'Vacye' as a house for the headmaster, and Radnor Lodge, which, like 'Ashfield', became accommodation for masters and their families. Its greatest financial operation at this time was the launching of a War Memorial Appeal of £100,000, just over half of which was raised. Part of the money was used for

---

* The Establishment is today called the Royal Radar Establishment.

Memorial Exhibitions for the sons of Old Malvernians who had lost their lives in the war.

Nos. 2 and 7 were not yet derequisitioned when the school returned to Malvern ; but Nos. 1, 8, and 9 were reopened in 1946 under H. C. W. Wilson, G. W. White, and J. S. Rambridge respectively. No. 1 consisted almost entirely of new boys at first; but Nos. 8 and 9 took their senior boys from other houses. No. 2 reopened in September 1947 under R. H. Bolam and No. 7 in September 1948 under G. L. M. Smith, both O.M.s. By that time almost all traces of T.R.E. occupation had vanished from the grounds, the demolition of the huts being at one stage vigorously assisted by the Youth Service Corps.

The rapid increase in numbers meant in the first years after the war a very young school and then later a very old school when all these boys reached senior status at the same time. There were many boys who would normally have been given positions of responsibility and who were frustrated by the fact that there is after all a limit to the number of house-prefects that one can make. Moreover, since the paramount need in the early days after the war was to raise numbers as quickly as possible, entrance standards were relaxed more than they would normally have been ; and these two factors between them were probably responsible for an unusual amount of rule-breaking and unpleasant incidents in 1951 and 1952. It also took some time before there was again a proper attitude to work. Standards of scholarship had been well maintained during the war : there were nine awards at Oxford and Cambridge in 1941 and again in 1945, and even now there were some quite good years ; but in 1949 Gaunt told the prefects that he was worried about the G.C.E. results and that at Christmas 'there were only five boys whose reports could be termed excellent'. At that time, in fact, some thirty per cent of the boys left without having a School Certificate.*

* It should, however, be remembered that, unlike the present-day General Certificate of Education, the old School Certificate required passes in five subjects.

All the same, it would be wrong to think that the boys were really apathetic to things of the mind. In 1950 six times as many books were drawn from the Grundy Library in one term than in the whole of 1948. The notice-boards were crowded with announcements of societies, some of which were short-lived, though others led a very active existence. Newcomers among the older established societies during Gaunt's Headmastership were a Fine Arts Society, a Gramophone Society, an Astronomical Society, a Sunday Discussion Group which talked about subjects related to Christianity, a Chess Club, a Modern Language Sixth Essay Club, a Madrigal Society, a Classical Society, and the Saturday Night Club which replaced the then defunct Allison Club with its aim of promoting self-entertainment. There was a Senior Scout Troop, an Aero Modelling Club, a Young Farmers' Club, a Campanological Group, a group of Sword Dancers and a Golf Society — in short, there was scope for the interests of almost every kind of boy. The Art Rooms at Malvern can never have been busier than during the short time between A. McClure's appointment as Art Master and the move to Blenheim. The *Malvernian* records that the following activities were available in the Art Rooms as hobbies : 'Drawing ; painting in oils, water-colours, and poster colours ; etching, drypoint, wood-engraving, lino-cutting, and colour-block printing ; modelling in clay and plaster ; sculpture — carving in stone, wood, and soap ; book-binding. A Stage Society is also in process of formation, by which it is hoped that boys will design, construct, and paint the scenery for the School play.'

On the musical side, the standard of piano playing and above all of choral work was always very high. Davison's swansong was a magnificent performance of the *Messiah* in Oxford Town Hall during the Blenheim days ; and that Easter Sunday the whole school sang the Hallelujah Chorus as an anthem in Woodstock Parish Church. When Davison left, Malvern music came under the guidance of that distinguished musician Julius Harrison. As has already been told,

Mr Havergal, the Harrow master, took charge of Malvern's singing on the Hill; and L. J. Blake, who was appointed shortly before the school returned to Malvern, has brought the most exacting standards to Malvern singing ever since. One of the casualties of the war, however, was the quality of Malvern's orchestral work, for there were simply not enough boys who played an instrument; and especially there was a shortage of string players, the backbone of any orchestra.

Theatricals had been suspended during the war; but the School Play was revived in 1945 and the Masters' Play on Shrove Tuesday in 1949. On Speech Day that year the school even performed '*L'Avare*' in French, partly as an additional tribute to the Free French Cadets, whose memorial was unveiled that same weekend in the presence of their former Commandant, Major Beaudoin.

All this variety of activities was faithfully reflected in the pages of the *Malvernian*, which in fact reached a higher quality than, with the exception of its earliest issues in the 1860s and 1870s, it had ever done before. The *Beacon* had faded out in 1936; a successor, the *Griffin*, had not been very successful; and from July 1939 to the reappearance of the *Beacon* in March 1947 the *Malvernian* gave a home in its columns to literary contributions which had previously gone to these little magazines and which now greatly livened up the record of the term's activities. War-time paper-shortage meant that the *Malvernian* could be published only once a term; and this was all to the good, since it is doubtful whether a high standard can be consistently achieved by a school magazine that appears more frequently than that. The unusual circumstances of a school in war-time evoked some fine writing, neither pompous nor flippant, and the editorials never again fell back to the trivialities from which they had begun to escape in the 1930s.

Games, of necessity, were hampered, first by the war and then by the youth of the school as numbers began to rise; but in 1949, which was A. H. Chadder's last year as master in charge of football, the Eleven won all four of its school matches, a fitting end to his inspiring and devoted work. Malvernian footballers of this period continued to win Blues at the universities afterwards and so did G. H. Chesterton for cricket. Chesterton came back to join the staff and take charge of the cricket in 1950. One other sporting achievement remains in the memories of many Old Malvernians : the Ledder of 1951, when R. H. Chadder of School House discovered a new route which gave School House seven of the nine Ledder caps.

A visible link with the sporting days of long ago was, until his death in 1953, 'Father' Tate. He had come to the school in 1903 after five years as a professional with the Hampshire county team. For the next twenty years he worked successively with Toppin, Fiddian-Green, and Chalk ; and on his retirement from active cricket in 1937 ran the School Store until his death. He had then been at the school seventeen years longer than anyone then at the College.

Another very popular College servant was J. H. Gunster, who had succeeded 'Charlie' as School Porter and who must have been the first friend that many a timid new boy found in the College. He created an aura of benignity around his office which his successor, Bob Drew — who will have served the College for fifty years in the Centenary Year — has maintained by his own unfailing kindliness. Sergeant-Major Wilson was with the school until it went to Harrow. He had all the classic features of the great sergeant-majors : the fierce waxed moustache, the ruddy cheeks, the swagger and panache, and a variety of voice from the blood-curdling parade-ground command to the *sotto voce* comment let slip from the side of the mouth ; but there was good humour behind it all. He had a great devotion to Malvern and lived to see the fulfilment of a great hope : to see his grandsons as boys at Malvern.

In 1946 R. A. Ker retired after thirty-five years as Bursar and Secretary to the College Council and was succeeded by Lieut.-Col. Murdoch-Cozens. In his early days, Ker had had much to do with the consolidation of the debt and then with the negotiations leading to the Royal Charter ; and in his later years much of the organization of two evacuations had fallen on his shoulders.

Of Major Elliott's herculean services to the school as Second Master during the evacuation to Blenheim something has already been said in the preceding pages. He left in 1942. 'Judy' Porch retired from the Staff in 1939, though this was by no means the end of his services to the school, since he continued to remain Secretary and Treasurer of the Malvernian Society until 1946 and became its President in 1956. He had come to the school as a boy in 1888 and since then had been away from Malvern for only ten years. What he did not know about the history of the school, the ways of boys and of men, and the lore of cricket was hardly worth knowing. Much of the material in the earlier chapters of this book is drawn from his reminiscences.

H. T. Gillmore retired in 1938 after thirty-nine years as Art master. A colleague writes, 'Schools often produce "characters", but I think they are frequently rather spurious or merely eccentric. Gillie was absolutely genuine. . . . He was a finely built man, with obvious Viking ancestry, fair curly hair and an untidy moustache. In his old age he grew a thick beard and looked more of a Highland chieftain than ever. As a young man he ran very wild — wine, women, and song — all of which he enjoyed with uninhibited gusto, and most of all poaching. He loved to tell stories of the tricks he had played on game-keepers and police in his lusty youth. As an artist he was of the school of Landseer : very exactly recorded dead pheasants and hares. If small enough, they were rather good. . . .'

O. Meade-King, housemaster of No. 4, retired in the same year as 'Gillie', after thirty-three years as a master at Malvern. After the war, too, the school had to say good-bye to a number of masters with long years of service : F. W. Roberts, who always learnt to recognize every boy in the school ; the gigantic M. C. Nokes, a brilliant scientist and adventurous teacher, always at work in the laboratories on experiments of his own, and amateur philosopher, glass-blower, and hammer thrower (at the Empire and Olympic Games) besides ; and H. M. Robinson, housemaster of No. 5, of whom a colleague writes, 'He and his wife by their warm-hearted friendliness found it easy to establish that easy human relationship, the natural friendship of housemaster and boys that is now so much more common than it was thirty years ago. . . . It is not by chance that nearly every O.M., however slightly he knew H.M.R. at school, goes to see him among the first every time he comes back to Malvern.'

Among masters who did not spend so many years of their life at Malvern, one in particular should be mentioned, for he afterwards scaled great heights : Wilfrid Noyce, a member of the expedition which climbed Mount Everest in 1953. He was tragically killed on the Anglo-Soviet climbing expedition in the Pamir mountains in 1962.

The College Council had three Chairmen during Gaunt's time. Lord Justice Lawrence retired in 1941 ; and the ninth Viscount Cobham, Lord-Lieutenant of the County and grandson of the Lord Lyttelton who had been a member of the first College Council in 1862, was Chairman during the difficult years from 1941 to his death in 1949. He was succeeded by a distinguished O.M., Sir Gerald Canny, who had been Chairman of the Board of Inland Revenue.

In 1953 Gaunt retired and soon afterwards took Holy Orders. No previous headmaster of Malvern College had been faced with such formidable difficulties : the first indications of another depression just before the war ; the transplanting of the organism that is a school three times in three years and then a fourth time four years later ; the uncertainties which during this period faced the public schools about their political future. The correspondence of Gaunt with the Government Departments during the weeks of the two requisitions show neither fluster nor self-pity, but a spirit which matched the hour.

These years, however, left their mark. Gaunt's longing
for a settled, traditional way of doing things after all these
upheavals remained part of him and scarcely diminished with
the years back at Malvern. He held a meeting with the school-
prefects every Sunday. Of one of these meetings during his
last term, the minutes record, 'He said that for the next three
weeks he was going to talk about traditions. This was
prompted by the fact that Mr Lindsay would be unfamiliar
with the traditions of this School. As a whole, human beings
dislike what they are unfamiliar with, and the Headmaster
illustrated this point with an anecdote of himself at Rugby
and Malvern.' What that anecdote was the minutes do not
say. Gaunt had indeed had more than his fair share of unfamiliar experiences since that first Speech Day two years
before the watershed of the war, when he had looked forward
to changes that the future would bring. Yet already boys
were entering the school who were too small when the war
ended to have any clear memories of it. The post-war generation was arriving.

CHAPTER IX

The Headmastership of D. D. Lindsay

DONALD LINDSAY was educated at Clifton and
Trinity College, Oxford. He has taught at Manchester
Grammar School, has been a lecturer in education at Bristol
University, Senior Historian at Repton, and then for eleven years
headmaster of Portsmouth Grammar School. He is perhaps
the first headmaster since Faber with a twinkle in his eye. He
takes his work seriously, but himself not at all. He leads by
encouragement. He drives neither his staff nor his boys;
fear and awe are not weapons in his armoury. It is characteristic of him that he wants boys sent up to his study for
good work and not for bad work; and because it is so clear
to everyone that he prefers to praise rather than to reprove,
his criticisms, when they do come, are all the more effective.
He is the least aloof of headmasters, and by his own example
has softened the rigidities of a public school hierarchy from
the headmaster's study right down to the smallest fag. The
seriousness underlying these attitudes is concealed behind a
screen of irreverent wit and light-hearted humour. The
prefects' minutes show that they found the new headmaster's
dicta irresistible; and it is a loss to the historian that in his
second term Lindsay asked that what he said at prefects'
meetings should no longer be recorded. He is incapable of
making a dull speech or of preaching a boring sermon. In
fact, he conceives the combating of dullness, apathy, or mere
routine as one of his chief functions; and his openness to
new ideas and willingness to experiment have imparted to the
school something of his own vitality.

After the return from Harrow at the end of the war, the first task facing the headmaster had been to fill the school. In the last chapter we have seen that this was done, but that the need for rapid expansion had led to a lowering of admission standards, which had had a poor effect on the academic standard of the school at the time and was dangerous for the future, since prep. school headmasters concluded that Malvern would take their weaker boys and were sometimes reluctant to send their better ones. Gaunt had already realized the prime importance of raising the quality of academic work and had started on this task. Although some very good men joined the staff after the war, he was hampered in attracting enough first-class teachers by a low salary scale ; and one of the first steps that Lindsay successfully urged on the Council was the need to improve salaries. He was firmly convinced that not only Malvern, but all public schools could survive in the post-war world only if they gave to academic work the absolute priority which it had not necessarily had before the war. It was not only a question of getting a good entry : equally important, at the other end, was the question of the universities. As government and county grants became available to anyone who secured admission to a university and as parental poverty ceased to be an absolute bar to university entry, the competition for places became increasingly severe, and public school boys of only moderate academic attainments could no longer count on getting to the universities. That their sons should get there was, however, still the ambition of a great number of parents who sent their boys to public schools ; so that on this score, too, the raising of standards at Malvern was imperative.

So Lindsay tried to instil a new sense of purpose and a new attitude to work into the school. His success in convincing the senior boys that this was now the most important objective is reflected by a series of editorials in the *Malvernian* which faithfully repeated his exhortations. On Speech Day of 1957 Lindsay was able to say, 'There is considerable evidence to

Photo by Norman May

D. D. LINDSAY, HEADMASTER SINCE 1953

show that throughout the School there is at any rate a grim acceptance if not a ready embrace of the necessity for some hard work'.

Two additional periods were added to the weekly time-table. More time was allocated to the preparation of work in 'Hall'. Monthly report cards were introduced. In 1955, rather than keep the school full by taking boys whose Common Entrance performance was bad, a slight but noticeable drop in numbers was deliberately accepted — an act which paid in the long run. In one year the number of 'O' level passes increased by over twenty per cent and went on improving in later years. By 1960 forty-five per cent of the school was in the Sixth Form — in 1939 it had been thirty-four per cent. The 'A' level results also began to improve, and there were some good years for university awards : eight in 1955/6, seven in 1961/2 — not outstanding when compared with the results of schools with a great academic tradition, but encouraging for a school that was trying to establish such a tradition.

A feature to be noticed about the expansion of the Sixth Forms was the increase in the proportion of boys on the Science side. When in 1955 F. Hare retired from the post of Senior Science Master, which he had held for twenty-eight years, he could look back on a period of tremendous growth in which, not only as a teacher but also as administrator of the Preston Science School Fund, he had played a vital part.

At one point in 1958 as many as sixty per cent of Sixth Formers were doing science subjects, compared with about forty per cent ten years earlier. The Preston Science School could not accommodate such numbers, and the school could not have undertaken a large building programme unaided. However, help came from industry. In 1955 a number of prominent manufacturing concerns set up the Industrial Fund for the Advancement of Scientific Education in Schools, with the aim of increasing facilities in Independent and Direct Grant Schools. Over £3 million were subscribed ; and of this £14,500 was in the first instance allocated to Malvern, on the understanding that the school would provide about half that sum in addition, and this was paid by the Malvernian Society. So a modern extension was built onto the Preston Science School ; and it was formally opened by Lord Weeks, the Treasurer of the Industrial Fund, in February 1958. Two years later the Fund offered a further gift of £6,000 towards the cost of adding another floor to the extension ; and the Malvernian Society contributed another £2,500 to enable the school to accept that offer, too. The handsome lecture room on the new floor was named the Salter Room, in memory of J. J. Salter, for many years head of the Chemistry Department and Housemaster of No. 6, who died suddenly that year.

The second gift of the Fund, coming so soon after the first, was certainly a recognition by industry of the work done by the Science Department at Malvern. In recent years a good deal of pioneering work in the teaching of science has gone on there. M. C. Nokes had been one of the first champions of the introduction of radioactivity work into the Physics syllabus. J. J. Salter had introduced semi-micro work, at that time still very much of an innovation, into the Chemistry teaching ; and J. L. Lewis, who became Senior Science Master in 1955, has given a further impetus to adventurous work in the laboratories. His interest in the expansion and modernization of the Physics taught in schools has brought him to the centre of what might be called the politics of science education in England. He has made visits to the United States, Germany, and the Soviet Union to study the organization and techniques of science teaching in those very science-conscious countries. He found there more modern syllabuses, more up-to-date methods, and a far more generous supply of expensive teaching equipment than schools generally enjoy in this country. When, at the suggestion of the Ministry of Education, the Science Masters' Association, one of the most active of teachers' organizations, set up a committee on the teaching of modern physics, he became its Chairman. Much of the experimental work connected with this project was actually done in the laboratories at Malvern, and the College was one of the thirty schools in a pilot scheme for teaching a new syllabus which includes aspects of modern physics not hitherto taught in schools.

But this new work required modern and expensive equipment which, for one reason or another, the Government could not finance. Industry has been most generous in supporting Malvern's pilot projects. The Industrial Fund added £1,800 for equipment to its first grant and a further £800 to its second. A number of firms have given additional equipment to the school. The most massive help has come from the Nuffield Foundation. This has given a quarter of a million pounds to finance projects by which a number of teams are working out improvements in the teaching of the different branches of science ; and Malvern provided the team responsible for that part of the Physics Project dealing with Quantum Phenomena (Modern Physics). In 1963 Lewis was appointed Associate Director of the Physics Project as a whole. More laboratory space was also needed at Malvern if all this research was to go on at the same time as the every-day science teaching ; and further gifts of money made possible the addition of a research wing to the Science block in 1964. All this has helped to make Malvern's laboratories the best-equipped and most up-to-date school laboratories in England, and the work done there has attracted attention not only at home, but also abroad. Scientists of many nationalities have found their way to Malvern and to No. 8 (where Lewis is housemaster) for meetings and discussions, and in 1962 the Malvern laboratories welcomed an international conference of physicists under the auspices of the Organization for Economic Cooperation and Development (O.E.C.D.) on whose Physics Committee Lewis is one of the British representatives.

Prep. schools of course often find even the simplest equipment too expensive, so that boys coming to public schools at the age of thirteen often have no knowledge of science at all (whereas in the Grammar Schools science teaching begins at eleven plus). To overcome this difficulty, Lewis persuaded the Esso Petroleum Company, which already had a scheme of lending scientific apparatus to Independent Secondary Schools, to extend this to prep. schools and to lend them a series of simple basic science kits, complete with instruction booklets on how to use them. Most of the kits and booklets have been designed and written by the science staff at Malvern, who have also conducted for the I.A.P.S. (Incorporated Association of Preparatory Schools) holiday courses on science teaching for preparatory school masters. It is perhaps fitting that all these contributions to the development of science in England should have come from the school which had been the home of Radar during the war.

Valuable experiments in education were also made in the Modern Language Department under A. I. Leng. Another generous grant from the Nuffield Foundation enabled Malvern to become in 1963 the first public school to have a Language Laboratory, equipped with glass-fronted booths in which boys listen through ear-phones to tapes and record their own answers, each boy working at his own speed, while a control panel enables the master to listen to and communicate with each boy individually. The method achieves extraordinary concentration, by means of which a fluency in spoken French, German, Spanish, and Russian is being acquired which neither bookwork nor even the old conversation lessons produced.

Strong as is his emphasis on academic work, nothing would appal a man of Lindsay's temperament more than that high academic standards should be achieved at the expense of the full life, whose realization must always remain the chief aim of a good education. Out-of-school activities became ever more numerous. New societies joined the already long list of the older established ones : among them a Spanish Society and a History Society, a Reels Club, an Angling Club and a Sailing Club whose members built their own sailing site on the Severn near Upton, a Theatre and a Jazz Club. At the German Society, Oscar Konstandt's 'Weihnachtsabende' in the Grub

were for years a gay and melodious prologue to Christmas
House Suppers. The 'Anti-Uglies' photographed eye-sores
in the town and sketched suggested improvements. The Film
Society showed classics of the cinema, and a group of boys
made a film of life at Malvern for the Centenary celebrations.
The Natural History Society had the good fortune that the
College was offered a Nature Reserve of 26 acres centred round
the house at Hope End which was once the home of Elizabeth
Barrett Browning. The Socratic Society and the Forum were
the old Sixth and Fifth Form Discussion Societies provided with
grander names ; and in their wake followed a number of discussion groups inside houses. Many of these societies by their
nature catered principally for the older boys ; and in 1956
something was done for boys in their first year, when they
often found it difficult to occupy themselves after the highly
organized life which they had led at their preparatory schools.
Called the Ferrets, the new boys went on expeditions, held hat
debates, had the occasional lecture or film show, divided into
groups for various hobbies, and from 1958 onwards staged a
play for the rest of the school in the summer term. For the
same group of boys the Pioneers began in 1956. While the
over-fourteens are in the Corps, these youngest boys in their
denims can be seen rope-climbing, map-reading, and going
in for other kinds of field-craft which test their ingenuity and
enterprise.

The training of boys in ingenuity and enterprise is something else to which Lindsay attaches great importance. Every
year after the 'A' level exams are over, there is an awkward
period before the end of term in which normal school routine
is looked on with a jaundiced eye by boys and masters alike.
From 1954 onwards some of this time was used by sending
boys off on expeditions all over the neighbouring counties
with certain tasks to perform within a limited time and all
requiring a good deal of resourcefulness. The report of these
tests in the *Malvernian* caught the eye of the authorities
responsible for working out the schemes for the Duke of

Edinburgh's Awards ; and consequently Sir John Hunt invited Malvern to be one of the schools to try out the schemes before they were launched officially. Apart from this, the initiative schemes were extended into Arduous Training. From 1957 onwards boys went off for long weekends to train in the Brecons before going on more prolonged camps in the Cairngorms during the holidays.

Lindsay is the first headmaster of Malvern who is not himself a games player ; but he knows very well the value of games and their importance in the life of any vigorous schoolboy. 'We are very fortunate at the moment in those masters who are in charge of games,' he said one Speech Day. 'They possess two essential but rare qualities in those who devote themselves to training boys to play games — a sense of proportion and a determination that games exist to be enjoyed by those who play them. Games at Malvern are neither a burden nor a compulsory religious exercise : moreover, the boy whose abilities lie elsewhere is not an outcast.'

It was a particularly successful period in the history of Malvern football under D. F. Saunders. In 1956, 1957, and 1960 the Eleven were unbeaten. At Oxford one O.M. captain, J. M. Costeloe, was succeeded by another, M. J. Theobald, in 1960. The Old Malvernians won the Arthur Dunn Cup in 1955 for the first time in eighteen years, and again in 1957. Malvern won the Quadrangular Boxing Competition (with Cheltenham, Clifton, and Downside) in 1959, 1960, and 1962 ; and the Triangular Athletics (with Shrewsbury and Cheltenham) in 1953, 1954, and 1960. In 1962 Malvern won the Schools Tetrathlon Competition at Sandhurst. The Rackets Courts were not released by T.R.E. until 1952. They were then badly in need of repair, the cost of which was generously met by H. J. Joel (O.M.), and play began again in 1953 for the first time since the move to Harrow eleven years before. Since 1956 coaching has been in the capable hands of Ron Hughes, who in 1963 became the first person to have held all the six major tennis trophies for professionals at the same time. In

1962 the squash facilities were extended by the building of two
additional courts behind the existing ones.

In addition to training the character, the intellect, and the
body, a good school must provide stimulus to the imagination
and the creative faculties. Drama and the arts have an important part to play here. There was a great expansion of
activity in theatricals, partly because Lindsay is himself a great
lover of the theatre. Apart from the annual School Play, the
Saturday Night Club produced *H.M.S. Pinafore* in 1953 ;
Green Pastures, the negro play for which a cast of about forty
small boys was blackened all over, began the run of the
Ferrets' Plays ; *The Vigil*, an Easter play, was movingly performed in the Chapel in 1959 ; and when School House put
on the first House Play for the rest of the school and it looked
as if other houses would want to follow suit, it became clear
that the time had come for a new departure. In 1960 took
place the first annual House Play Competition, in which the
various entries are entirely the work of the boys : indeed the
prize that year went to the performance of No. 8 in a play
which had been written by its producer, T. F. Keyes. Meanwhile the Masters' Shrove Tuesday Play, though still light-
hearted, became increasingly professional, and no boy who
saw them will forget the Reviews of 1957 and 1962. There
cannot be many headmasters who would dare or could afford
to appear before their school as the *prima ballerina* in a *corps
de ballet* composed of all the heftiest members of the staff !
Throughout the year there are numerous expeditions to the
theatre in Stratford, Birmingham, or Cheltenham ; and for a
while reviews of these performances appeared in the *Malvernian*.

The *Beacon* was once again and finally merged with the
Malvernian in 1954, so that the school magazine again became
a vehicle for the literary work of the boys. Besides essays,
poems, and reviews, there were accounts of the many school
parties which went abroad to ski, to play football, to give
exhibitions of sword-dancing, or to attend courses in Paris.
There are almost annual articles in which one of the American

Exchange Students, who began coming to Malvern for a year's work in the Sixth Form in 1954, relates how life at an English public school strikes an American. A growing number of houses began to produce their own house-magazines. School House's *Magpie* was joined by No. 6's *Bodger*, and by No. 5's highbrow *Theme*. No. 9's *Free Speech*, *Pieces of Eight* from No. 8, No. 4's *Hawk*, No. 7's *Outlook*, and No. 2's *Thought* also appeared, though rather less regularly.

One feature of this literary output is the amount of space that was given to discussion of the arts, in which interest was becoming increasingly active. The meetings of the Art Society presided over by the robustly provocative Art master, Harry Fabian Ware, and his enterprising successor, William Wilkins (O.M.), were among the liveliest in the school. The teaching of sculpture, which Miss Hilary Carruthers began in a small room in the Monastery in 1958, soon had to move to the ampler space of the old Museum and is now done by 'Gillie's' granddaughter, Miss Ann Gillmore. Pottery classes began in 1964 ; and in the same year the boys began to operate a printing press. Fine woodwork was also being done : the boys, for example, made the simple but very beautiful altar and rails for the little private chapel which, in 1962, was made in the vault under the main chapel. The corridors of the main building were ornamented with paintings and murals tending towards the fauve and with sculptures tending towards the abstract. These forms of art duly provoked discussion, controversy, and growing interest in the school. The Bursar, Lieutenant-Commander Merriman, had already banished the depressing institutional greens and browns from class-rooms, corridors, and houses. 'Ice blue, mist grey, and cardinal red have worked wonders', as Lindsay said one Speech Day ; and now in addition houses and some class-rooms were brightened with art reproductions as well. In 1962 a fund was started with which houses would buy original paintings and lithographs.*

---

* The fund consisted of a termly 2/6 on the bills to replace the charge for the 'Saturday bobs' — the shilling given to each boy on Saturdays, a survival

There was one full orchestral concert in 1955, two in 1959, one in 1963 (which also marked the debut of the C.C.F. military band), and one in 1964, but in most years the orchestral side of the school still suffered from a shortage of string players. The choral work, on the other hand, went on from strength to strength. In 1955 the Remembrance Day service was broadcast from the School Chapel. From 1957 onwards, the College combined each year with one of the girls' schools in or near Malvern for the choral concert in the Easter Term. This was not the only joint activity with the girls' schools. The Reels Club had been the first to establish contact ; later there were joint debates ; and regular dances began in 1961. An operetta, *The Batsman's Bride*, performed jointly by No. 8 and Ellerslie Girls' School in the summer of 1963, was followed later in the year by the two schools having a joint school play — Shaw's *Caesar and Cleopatra*. The restrictions on informal contacts have also been somewhat relaxed, so that the school is a little less monastic than it used to be.

Lindsay knows that a closely-knit and self-contained community like a public school runs a great danger of isolating itself from the rapidly changing world outside its walls. He has tried to make the boys aware of this in a number of ways : in his own speeches ('the world does not owe you a living just because you have been to a public school', he reminds them at frequent intervals) ; by inviting to the fortnightly Sixth Form lectures which he has introduced outside speakers with forthright views about the world in which we live ; by promoting weekend exchanges between Malvern boys and boys from Grammar and Comprehensive Schools. The Mission in Canning Town, indeed, was wound up in 1957. 'The twentieth century is suspicious of charity,' Lindsay wrote when explaining this step, 'and anything savouring of patronage is likely to do more harm than good. While it remains true that a Malvern boy has much to give to those brought up

from the very distant days when that sum was meant to cover his normal purchases during the week.

in a very different environment, it is equally true that he has a great deal to learn. It is increasingly the view of head-masters that the future of social work lies less in "charity" and far more in learning about each other. . . . To put this into practice it is essential that the distance between school and "mission" is not too great. Only by frequent contacts can any good be done.' Eventually regular visits to a Boys' Club in Pershore and activities with the Priory Youth Club in Malvern provided these contacts, whilst a scheme of Voluntary Service — visiting and helping elderly or handicapped people in the town, or providing manual labour for the tending of the Malvern Hills — met with a ready response. In all these ways the boys' social outlook has been widened somewhat ; and politically, a mock election at the time of the 1959 General Election, though still giving the Conservatives a comfortable lead, found the other parties being respectably supported.

If boys are encouraged not to take the privileges of the middle classes simply for granted, it can be expected that they might in course of time examine the hierarchy they have created among themselves and the methods by which this has been done ; and in this, too, they have had some prompting from Lindsay and his housemasters. The new boys' exam has ceased to inspire terror ; fag calls have been restricted to certain times of the day ; beatings by prefects are extremely rare and can be given only with housemasters' approval ; bullying is checked as soon as discovered. For some time prefects' meetings still gave a great deal of attention to the dress rules by which the seniority of a boy could be recognized. At one meeting in 1961 most of these were swept away.* Whilst in earlier decades new boys had found their first terms at their public school actually more restrictive than the life they had left behind at their prep. schools, they now find they have more scope and freedom than they had before, which is

---

* In the Centenary Year the old school uniform with its black jackets will disappear altogether, to be replaced with grey suits and house ties. The straw hats or 'bashers' will go at the same time.

of course as it should be. Prefects have on the whole been less inclined to buttress their own dignity with rules which were designed to take away that of the 'inferiors' (as they are still called) ; and although the earlier physical maturing of boys has not brought about in every respect a corresponding earlier psychological maturity, there is no doubt that one of its effects is that restrictions, whether obeyed or imposed, are critically examined at an earlier age than they used to be. Lindsay has always taken this into account, and where he has thought that a greater freedom could reasonably be given, especially to senior boys, he has done so.

It can be seen from this account that Lindsay gives constant thought to the challenges that modern society puts to the educationalist ; and one of these concerns the place of religious education. The Headmaster writes, 'Today this challenge presents itself in two ways : What is the place of a religious foundation in a secular society ? And how does one make sure that worship in a school chapel is not isolated from the accepted practices of the Church as a whole ? On the one hand there is now at Malvern only one compulsory service on Sundays, and House prayers do not take place on every evening of the week. On the other hand, in an attempt to make the religious life relevant to modern needs, much thought has been given to involving boys more closely with the conduct of Chapel services and to trying to meet views expressed through the Chapel Committee. Occasionally in the Lent Term each House is responsible for the content of one week's morning Chapel, and voluntary evening services have been conducted by boys themselves. Most important of all has been the deliberate attempt to ensure that what was once known as "public school religion" does not continue, and that Malvern Chapel should be not a department of school life but part of the world-wide Church. To this end, both in worship and in teaching, boys are trained to recognize the service of Holy Communion as the heart of Christian worship.' From the attendance at voluntary services one could conclude that worship is meaningful to a greater proportion of the school community than of the world outside.

Inevitably the years saw the retirement of a number of masters who had served the school for many years. References have been made elsewhere in these pages to F. Hare, C. A. F. Fiddian-Green, O. Konstandt, C. B. Lace, H. Fabian Ware, and J. S. Rambridge. Three Malvern masters left to become headmasters : D. W. Erskine became Rector of Dundee High School in 1955 ; D. E. Norfolk headmaster of Kent College, Canterbury, in 1960 ; and G. V. Surtees headmaster of Rishworth School, Halifax, in 1964. In 1962 R. T. Colthurst retired. He had succeeded F. H. Hooper as Second Master in 1948 and had acted as headmaster for a whole term in 1950, when Gaunt had been away ill. His last sermon in Chapel, on Courage, Honesty, and Purity, while giving expression to the standards of absolute integrity which his whole life exemplified, did not indicate the gentler virtues for which he is held in such affection : his courtesy, which is not a mere outward form, but a way of thought ; his liberalism, which enables him to be ever progressive without being 'advanced' ; the modesty which is his almost to a fault. To a brasher age, he was a constant reminder of the meaning of the word 'civilized'.

Other familiar Malvern figures who retired during these years included J. G. Brebber, the Estate Steward, who, long before the end of his thirty years at the College, was said to know every chimney stack and every drain throughout the extensive grounds ; and three Sergeant Instructors who had each given many years of devoted service to the Corps : Sgt. Major Harper, Q.M.S.I. Gasson, and R.S.M. Passfield. Since the departure of R.S.M. Passfield there has been only one Permanent Staff Instructor instead of two as in the past ; for his leaving coincided in time with a decision by the Services to reduce the numbers in the C.C.F. by laying down that in general boys should spend three years instead of four or five in the Corps. Since 1963 boys in their first year at school have therefore been free to spend one afternoon a week on arts and crafts ; the Pioneers have been moved to the second year ; and only at the beginning of his third year does a boy now enter the Army, R.N., or R.A.F. Section of the Corps.

Sir Gerald Canny died in 1954 and was succeeded as Chairman of the College Council by Admiral Sir William Tennant. Admiral Tennant had had a distinguished naval career which included the supervision of the evacuation from Dunkirk and playing a vital part in the planning of the invasion of Normandy. He was Lord-Lieutenant of the County ; and as he lived nearby at Upton-on-Severn, he was able to take an exceptionally close and detailed interest in every aspect of the school's life. He continued to serve on several sub-committees of the Council after he became Chairman ; and he was particularly concerned that the Houses should be modernized, that the grounds should be as beautiful as possible, and that relations between the Council and the masters should be close and cordial. His death in 1963 deprived the College of a Chairman who had given himself unstintedly to the school. He was succeeded by Sir John Wheeler-Bennett, the distinguished historian and Historical Adviser to the Royal Archives.

In May 1963 there was a record number of 600 boys in the school. The fact that the College was full to capacity was of great help in a period in which rising costs were constantly wiping out the additional income derived from increases in fees. Between 1955 and 1962 these had risen in five instalments from £276 a year to £465 ; but expenses had risen as fast. In addition, structural repairs to some of the older houses could not be put off any longer. Nos. 1 and 2, hastily built in the earliest days of the school's history, needed particularly extensive repairs ; and between 1948 and 1959 no fewer than forty-eight areas of dry rot in the College buildings had to be dealt with. In 1956 there were two outbreaks of fire in the Main Buildings. The first, in October, badly damaged the Headmaster's Study. The second, in December, was even more serious, for it destroyed a large part of the Grundy Library. When this room in the South Wing had been repaired, it became the new home of the Art School ; and the Grundy Library moved upstairs to the more spacious room which the Art School had previously occupied. Money from the insurance company and generous contributions from Old Malvernians helped to make this new Grundy Library one of the finest rooms in the school. After it had been formally opened by Sir John Wheeler-Bennett in February 1958, more boys came to read, work, and browse in it than had ever gone to the Old Grundy, much as this had been used in the years after the war. The lower room became a reference library and is now known as the Dyson Perrins Room, in memory of C. W. Dyson Perrins, one of the school's most munificent benefactors, who died in 1958, and in gratitude for a gift of £1,000 from his widow.

The Malvernian Society also contributed to this as to so many other building projects during this period. In addition, it launched a special drive in 1955 to buy in the then remaining £66,000 of debentures by the time of the Centenary in 1965; and this large task, the beginnings of which date back to 1918, was all but accomplished as this book went to press.

Yet no school can be entirely free of financial worries if it has nothing except its income to fall back on. To provide the College with an endowment that would give that extra security, a Centenary Appeal Fund was launched in June 1959. The original target was not less than £150,000. The response from Old Malvernians, beginning with a donation of £10,000 from H. J. Joel, was yet another indication that there can be few schools with as devoted and loyal a body of Old Boys. In the first year alone £112,000 was subscribed, and the provisional target was reached by April 1962. The response had already encouraged the Appeal Committee to fix the final target at £250,000. With such a sum behind it, Malvern could indeed feel confident that there will be no serious economic brakes on its progress as it enters its second century.

This is not the place to speculate on how politics may affect the progress of Malvern and other public schools in the years ahead. Masters and boys know that what these schools stand for — scholarship, service, loyalty, leadership, faith — are as true and as urgently needed today as they have ever been. They know that these qualities are not the exclusive property of the independent schools. They are aware that a condition of survival is that the public schools should look forward and should remain closely in touch with the world outside its walls. They feel confident that schools like Malvern can meet these demands and have as much to contribute as ever they had. They hope that when changes come, as come they will, they will not for political reasons destroy but rather maintain and enlarge what is educationally valuable in the public school system. Malvern will welcome any changes that will enable it to go on playing a worth-while part in a rapidly changing world.

THE HOUSES

School House

1865 Rev. A. Faber's private residence

1871 Faber becomes Housemaster in No. 3
School House renamed College House and houses assistant masters

1876 Rev. A. W. H. Howard begins to turn it into a boarding-house. Leaves later that year through ill health

1877 Faber takes over the House, now again called School House

1881 Rev. C. T. Cruttwell

1885 Rev. W. Grundy

1892 Rev. A. St. J. Gray

1897 Rev. S. R. James

1914 F. S. Preston

1937 H. C. A. Gaunt

1942 D. W. Erskine — later Rector of Dundee High School

1956 L. R. Dodd (O.M.)

1960 A. I. Leng

No. 1

1865 Rev. Charles McDowall — later headmaster of Highgate

1874 Rev. T. H. Belcher — later headmaster of Brighton College

1881 Rev. G. E. Mackie — later headmaster of Godolphin School, London

1887 Rev. H. M. Faber

1913 D. J. P. Berridge

1927 F. W. Roberts

1940 House merged with No. 8

1946 H. C. W. Wilson

1962 N. Rosser

No. 2

1865 Rev. F. R. Drew

1881 C. Graham
1883 Rev. M. A. Bayfield — later headmaster of Christ's College, Brecon and then of Eastbourne College
1890 J. N. Swann
1912 W. Greenstock
1927 P. E. A. Morshead
1940 Merged with No. 6
1947 R. H. Bolam (O.M.)
1960 G. V. Surtees
1964 J. M. McNevin

No. 3
1867 Rev. W. H. Maddock
1871 The Headmaster, Rev. A. Faber. House called School House
1877 Rev. T. Spear. House again called No. 3
1912 P. R. Farrant
1919 R. B. Porch (O.M.)
1933 Rev. W. O. Cosgrove
1951 M. A. Staniforth

No. 4
1868 Rev. L. Estridge
1878 Rev. E. L. Bryans
1889 Rev. H. E. Huntington (O.M.)
1893 H. H. House
1924 O. Meade-King
1938 A. H. Chadder
1956 Rev. R. G. Born

No. 5
1871 Rev. H. Foster (in what is now No. 6)
1908 L. S. Milward (O.M.). Moves into the present No. 5
1915 F. U. Mugliston
1927 H. M. Robinson
1940 Merges with No. 7
1946 R. T. Colthurst
1949 J. Collinson
1961 G. H. Chesterton

No. 6

1891 H. W. Smith, in 'Malvernbury'

1892 C. Toppin. Moves to present No. 5 in 1894, to present No. 6 in 1908

1925 Major H. D. E. Elliott

1938 J. J. Salter

1956 H. J. Farebrother

No. 7

1892 R. E. Lyon (O.M.) (Unofficially 1889)
  O. Meade-King *locum tenens* during the war

1925 Rev. C. E. Storrs (O.M.) — later Bishop of Grafton, N.S.W.

1930 R. T. Colthurst

1948 G. L. M. Smith

1962 D. F. Saunders

No. 8

1895 C. T. Salisbury, in 'Malvernhurst' ; in 'Malvernbury' 1903 ; in Radnor House 1906

1913 W. W. Lowe (O.M.)

1932 M. C. Nokes

1940 F. W. Roberts

1942 House dissolved

1946 G. W. White

1961 J. L. Lewis (O.M.)

No. 9

1898 E. C. Bullock (O.M.), in 'Cranhill' ; in 'Malvernbury' 1899 ; in Roslin House 1903
  G. G. Fraser *locum tenens* during the war

1917 G. G. Fraser (O.M.)

1927 F. H. Hooper (O.M.)

1942 House dissolved

1946 J. S. Rambridge

1961 R. A. Stobbs

CHAIRMEN OF THE COLLEGE COUNCIL

1863–1891 The sixth Earl Beauchamp
1891–1905 G. E. Martin
1905–1918 The seventh Earl Beauchamp
1919–1941 Lord Justice Lawrence
1941–1949 The ninth Viscount Cobham
1950–1954 Sir Gerald Canny
1954–1963 Admiral Sir William Tennant
1964–   Sir John Wheeler-Bennett

THE CARMEN IN ENGLISH

Ho ! Comrades, hearts and voices raise,
To welcome summer holidays ;
Away with books, tear up the 'scheme' ;
No thoughts of these to spoil our dream !
    Come, Alma Mater, let us sing
    Till overhead the rafters ring
    With her — 'tis hers — our glory sharing
    With answering love our love declaring. *

Of Thames let Eton boast her fill,
And Harrow glory in her hill ;
But Malvern's mountains reach the sky,
And bounteous health her streams supply.

Whether we roam the smiling plain,
Or toil those storied heights to gain,
What fairer scene shall any find
To breed both healthy frame and mind ?

Thus strengthened by our Mother's might,
Both Past and Present now unite
With loyal hearts, a vigorous band,
To spread her fame in every land.

Thorough in work and keen in games,
Nor yet neglecting virtue's claims,
If aught of good we here have won,
Hers be the praise and hers alone !

* The first two lines of the chorus in Latin used to be :
        Age, fratres, (sic eamus),
        Almam Matrem canamus.

Hurrah ! Hurrah !
Elevens both, a cheer for you,
And for our gallant marksmen, too,
And you who guard with skill and zeal
At Prince's Court the common weal !

Hurrah ! Hurrah !
Our Gymnasts cheer ; cheer them whose fame
Is to have won a scholar's name ;
A cheer for all whose feats renowned
Their own and Malvern's praise resound !

Hurrah ! Hurrah !
A health to all, — the Guiding hand
And each one of the gownèd band ;
To Old Boys' cherished memory,
To all Malvernians yet to be.

THE CHAPEL GLASS

FROM the introduction to the *Malvern College Register, 1865 to 1914*:
Dr. Montague James, Provost of King's College, Cambridge,*
was asked to draw up a scheme for filling all the windows with
stained glass. His scheme provided that the East window and the
large windows on the North and South sides should illustrate the
Christian Year from Advent to All Saints' Day, the upper halves of
the latter windows shewing types from the Old Testament, the lower
half the fulfilment of those types in the New Testament; the
East Window should represent the Crucifixion, and Christ en-
throned in glory. The execution of the designs for these windows,
as they should be from time to time provided, was entrusted to
Messrs C. E. Kempe & Co., with extremely successful results. The
East window commemorates the Malvernians who fell in the South
African War, and a brass tablet giving their names has been placed
in the Ante-Chapel below a window which also forms part of the
same memorial. On the South side one window bears the legend,
Matres alumnorum posuerunt, another was given by Mr E. F. Chance
in memory of his father, who was a member of the Council, and
three are in memory of Canon Loraine Estridge, T. W. Barker,
and Evelyn Charrington. On the North side are memorial windows
to the Rev. W. Grundy and W. H. B. Evans.† Six of the windows
in the aisle were transferred from the old Chapel, and are in memory
of Mrs Faber, the wife of the first headmaster, and J. J. Bell; the
two remaining windows are memorials to Herbert Ingleby and
Captain Michael Lindsay. Some memorial tablets were also transferred from the old Chapel, and the size and shape of all such tablets
were fixed for the future.

* He was the brother of S. R. James and is well known to a large public
today as M. R. James, the author of many ghost stories. He also played a
leading part in the restoration and rearrangement of the mediaeval glass in
Malvern Priory. (Smith, *op. cit.* Chapter XII.)

† Since 1914 memorial windows have been added on the north side to
Faber, James, and Foster.

SOURCES

A. Private Sources

Minutes of the Council of Malvern College

Annual Reports of the Council of Malvern College

Minutes of the Malvernian Society

Four editions of the *Malvern College Register*, and two Supplements
thereto

A MS. diary of school affairs kept by the Rev. Arthur Faber and
continued for a time by the Rev. C. T. Cruttwell : two vols.

A typescript by F. S. Preston on his Headmastership

Volumes of *The Malvernian*

Various boxes of papers and documents in the office of Malvern
College

Some 150 letters from Old Malvernians and others

Two books of newspaper cuttings

B. Newspapers, Periodicals, etc.

The Malvern News

The Malvern Advertiser

The Malvern Gazette

Berrows Worcester Journal

The Field

The Illustrated Sporting and Dramatic News

The Harrovian

C. Books

Arlen, Michael — *Piracy* (Collins, 1922)

De Zouche, Dorothy E. — *Roedean School, 1885 to 1955* (Printed
Privately, 1955)

Gaunt, H. C. A. — *Two Exiles* (Sampson Low, Marston & Co.,
Ltd., 1946)

Appendix E

Greene, Graham (ed.) — *The Old School* (Cape, 1934)

Hammond, N. G. L. (ed.) — *Centenary Essays on Clifton College* (Arrowsmith, 1962)

Holmes, E. R. T. — *Flannelled Foolishness* (Hollis & Carter, 1957)

James, S. R. — *Seventy Years* (Williams & Norgate, 1926)

Johnstone, S. M. — *The History of the King's School, Parramatta* (1932)

Kennedy-Cox, Sir Reginald — *An Autobiography* (Hodder & Stoughton, 1931)

Leach, A. F. — *A History of Warwick School* (Constable, 1906)

Lewis, C. S. — *Surprised by Joy* (Bles, 1955)

Mack, E. C. — *Public Schools and British Opinion, 1780 to 1860* (Methuen, 1938)

Mack, E. C. — *Public Schools and British Opinion Since 1860* (Columbia U.P., 1941)

McVeagh, Diana M. — *Edward Elgar* (Dent, 1955)

Newsome, David — *A History of Wellington College* (Murray, 1959)

Newsome, David — *Godliness and Good Learning* (Murray, 1961)

Ogilvie, Vivien — *The English Public School* (Batsford, 1957)

Pelham, Sir Henry (ed.) — *Public Schools Cricket, 1901 to 1950* (Parrish, 1957)

Rowe, A. P. — *One Story of Radar* (C.U.P., 1948)

Severn Burrows, C. F. — *A Little City Set on a Hill* (1948)

Smith, Brian S. — *History of Malvern* (Leicester U.P., 1964)

Walters, R. C. S. — *The Nation's Water Supply* (Nicholson & Watson, 1936)

Who's Who and *Who Was Who* — various editions

Wodehouse, P. G. — *Mike at Wrykyn* (Herbert Jenkins, 1953)

NOTES

Chapter I

1   R. C. S. Walters, *The Nation's Water Supply*, p. 154
2   Brian S. Smith, *History of Malvern*, chapters 10 and 11
3   *Malvern Gazette*, January 17, 1913
4   E. L. Bryans in the *Malvern Register*, I, xix
5   See E. C. Mack, *Public Schools and British Opinion Since 1860*, chapters I, II, III
6   See John Betjeman on the Clifton College Buildings, in *Centenary Essays on Clifton College*
7   The Rev. E. L. Bryans. See *The Malvernian*, October 1889
8   *Berrows Worcester Journal*, July 18, 1863
9   *Ibid.* July 25, 1863
10 *Malvern News*, February 1, 1868
11 *Malvern Advertiser*, May 14, 1864

Chapter II

1   *The Field*, December 3, 1910
2   From the eighth Annual Report
3   E. L. Bryans, *Malvern Register*, I, xxxviii
4   *Berrows Worcester Journal*, July 25, 1863
5   Mack, *Public Schools and British Opinion, 1780 to 1860*, p. 359
6   *Malvern Register*, I, lvii
7   *The Malvernian*, December 1888
8   See Ogilvie, *The English Public School*, pp. 148-151
9   *Malvern College Register*, III, xv

Chapter III

1   *Malvern Register*, III, xvii

Chapter IV

1   A. F. Leach, *History of Warwick School*, p. 217
2   I, xlii
3   *Pall Mall Gazette*, November 28, 1892
4   Smith, *op. cit.* chapter xi
5   *Pall Mall Gazette*, November 28, 1892

Notes

CHAPTER V

1 *The Malvernian,* July 1896
2 Sir Reginald Kennedy-Cox, *An Autobiography,* p. 43

CHAPTER VI

1 *Seventy Years,* p. 134
2 *Ibid.* p. 121
3 *Ibid.* pp. 110, 183
4 *Illustrated Sporting and Dramatic News,* June 7, 1935
5 *Flannelled Foolishness,* p. 13
6 *Surprised by Joy,* p. 98
7 *Ibid.* pp. 109 ff.
8 *Flannelled Foolishness,* pp. 12 to 15
9 *Public School Cricket,* p. 104
10 Sir Reginald Kennedy-Cox, *An Autobiography,* p. 121
11 For Kennedy-Cox's lively campaign against drink, see *op. cit.* pp. 127 to 136
12 *Op. cit.* p. 92
13 *Op. cit.* p. 106
14 *Seventy Years,* p. 147
15 C. S. Lewis, *op. cit.* p. 98
16 See David Newsome, *Godliness and Good Learning,* chapter 4, and especially p. 200. The chapter is entitled 'Godliness and Manliness' and traces the development of the encouragement of 'muscular Christianity' in the late Victorian schools.
17 *Seventy Years,* p. 145

CHAPTER VII

1 See *The Malvernian,* No. ccclx
2 *The Work of the Malvernian Society,* published July 1950
3 D. J. Knight in *Public Schools Cricket, 1901–1950,* ed. Sir Pelham Warner. I owe much of this and the previous paragraph to his chapter and to E. W. Swanton's article on Malvern cricket in the *Illustrated Sporting and Dramatic News* of June 7, 1935
4 D. J. Knight, *op. cit.*

CHAPTER VIII

1 R.T.C. in the *Malvernian.* December 1939
2 *The Malvernian,* July 1941
3 *Ibid.* December 1942
4 *Ibid.* December 1945
5 *One Story of Radar,* p. 95
6 *Ibid.* p. 137

INDEX

Allison, R., 108
Anderson, C. V., 92
Anderson, D. A. P., 137
Anderson, Sir John, 137
Arnold, T., 1, 17
Arber, G., 40, 81, 113
Arlen, M., *see* Kouyoumdjian
Army Side, 32, 102
Art, 155, 170
Ashfield, 98 n., 153
Athletics, 113, 168

Baddeley, Hermione, 55
Baldwin, S., 70, 82, 105, 122, 123
Banks, M. L., 54, 64
Barker, C. D., 67, 69
Barnes, Sir Hugh Shakespeare, 83
Bayfield, M. A., 34
Beacon, The, 104, 156, 169
Beauchamp, *see* Lygon
Beaudoin (Major), 156
Beeson, N. W., 113
Belcher, T. H., 29, 30
Benson, Sir Frank, 49, 50 n.
Berridge, D. J. P., 43, 46, 61, 119
Bird, W. S., 51
Blake, L. J., 156
Blenheim, 125 ff.
Blomfield, Sir Arthur, 43, 68
Blomfield, C. J., 68
Boer War, 77, 89
Boissier, A. P., 139, 140, 144
Bolam, R. H., 154
Bowket, 15
Boxing, 113, 168
Bracken, Sir Geoffrey, 83
Bradfield, 28
Bradshaw, W. H., 112
Braithwaite, C., 69
Brayne-Baker, F., 120
Brebber, J. H., 174
Brodhurst, A. H., 112
Bromley-Martin, G. E., 48 n.
Browning, Elizabeth Barrett, 167
Bruton, E., 120
Building Company, 10, 23, 24, 25, 33

Bullock, E. C., 32, 33, 46, 66, 67, 82 n., 85 n., 87, 110 n., 119
Burnup, C. J., 38
Burrow, H. H., 3, 5
Burrow, J., 3, 4
Burrow, W., 3, 4, 6
Burton, R. C., 56
Butler, R. A., 137, 140, 145
Butler, S., 1

Canny, Sir Gerald, 159, 175
Capes, C. J., 112
Carlyle, T., 2
Carmen, The, 34
Carruthers, Hilary, 170
Chadder, A. H., 140, 156
Chadder, R. H., 157
Chalk, F. G. H., 149, 157
Chapel, 8, 9, 12, 19, 34, 42, 43, 47, 68, 90, 143, 148, 173
Charterhouse, 1
Chase School, 153
Cheltenham College, 2, 3, 4, 24, 25, 113, 168
Chesterton, G. H., 157
Churchill, John, Duke of Marlborough, 130
Churchill, Lord Randolph, 34
Churchill, Sir Winston, 130, 131, 144
City of London School, 138
Classics, 5, 34, 57, 101, 102
Clifton College, 6, 25, 113, 161, 168
Clutterbuck, Sir Alexander, 101 n.
Cobham, *see* Lyttelton
Cody, S. F., 51
Cohen, Sir Andrew, 83
Collett, A. P., 82
Colthurst, R. T., 140, 174
Conant, R. J. E., 149
Constitution, 12, 69, 70, 85, 86, 97, 98
Cooke, A. H., 48
Cookson, R. T. C., 120
Corps, 24, 38, 39, 62, 78, 79, 80, 87, 114, 135, 174, 175
Cosgrove, W. O., 140

Index

Index

PRINTED BY R. & R. CLARK, LTD., EDINBURGH